BEI GRIN MACHT SICH IF WISSEN BEZAHLT

- Wir veröffentlichen Ihre Hausarbeit, Bachelor- und Masterarbeit

- Ihr eigenes eBook und Buch - weltweit in allen wichtigen Shops

- Verdienen Sie an jedem Verkauf

Jetzt bei www.GRIN.com hochladen und kostenlos publizieren

Geschlechtsbezogene Stereotype und Diskriminierung. Möglichkeiten der Prävention und Intervention von Diskriminierung von Schülerinnen aufgrund ihres Geschlechts

Luzie Fiest

Bibliografische Information der Deutschen Nationalbibliothek:

Die Deutsche Nationalbibliothek verzeichnet diese Publikation in der Deutschen Nationalbibliografie; detaillierte bibliografische Daten sind im Internet über http://dnb.d-nb.de abrufbar.

ISBN: 9783346904034
Dieses Buch ist auch als E-Book erhältlich.

© GRIN Publishing GmbH
Trappentreustraße 1
80339 München

Druck und Bindung: Books on Demand GmbH, Norderstedt Germany
Gedruckt auf säurefreiem Papier aus verantwortungsvollen Quellen

Das vorliegende Werk wurde sorgfältig erarbeitet. Dennoch übernehmen Autoren und Verlag für die Richtigkeit von Angaben, Hinweisen, Links und Ratschlägen sowie eventuelle Druckfehler keine Haftung.

Das Buch bei GRIN: https://www.grin.com/document/1370556

Martin-Luther-Universität Halle-Wittenberg
Philosophische Fakultät III
Wintersemester 2022/23

Geschlechtsbezogene Stereotype und Diskriminierung – Möglichkeiten der Prävention und Intervention von Diskriminierung von Schülerinnen aufgrund ihres Geschlechts

Inhaltsverzeichnis

1. Einleitung

Jungen gelten heute noch als die „Bildungsverlierer" in der Schule.[1] Die Mädchen dagegen werden in der aktuellen Forschung wenig thematisiert, weshalb sie stets im Hintergrund der wissenschaftlichen Expertisen liegen.[2] Studien zeigen jedoch, dass Mädchen mittlerweile deutlich öfter eine Gymnasialempfehlung erhalten als Jungen, weshalb sie als „Bildungsgewinnerinnen" abgestempelt werden.[3] Betrachtet man allerdings den historischen Hintergrund stellt sich die Frage, ob die Mädchen heute wirklich zu den „Bildungsgewinnerinnen" zählen können und sich innerhalb eines Jahrhundert so viel geändert hat.

Im 20. Jahrhundert sah dies nämlich ganz anders aus, denn bis 1908 durften Mädchen überhaupt nicht zur Schule gehen und mussten ihrer Mutter im Haushalt helfen.[4] Ihnen blieb die Bildung verwehrt und selbst als sie dann schließlich in die Schule gehen durften, wurden sie an Mädchenschulen unterrichtet.[5] Auch die Unterrichtsthemen waren an die Geschlechter angepasst, sodass die Mädchen Unterricht in Handarbeiten, Religion und Hauswirtschaft erhielten.[6] Erst in den 1950er- und 1960er- Jahren gab es einen Wandel, denn durch die „Bildungsexpansion" entwickelte sich ein neues Bildungsbewusstsein in der gesamten Bevölkerung.[7] Die Bildungsbeteiligung von Jungen und Mädchen glich sich in den Folgejahren an und es wurden neue Schulen gebaut, sodass nun auch Mädchen die Möglichkeit auf die gleiche Bildung bekamen wie die Jungen.[8] Doch auch im 21. Jahrhundert lassen sich anhand der Schulnoten noch immer Unterschiede zwischen den Geschlechtern erkennen. So gelten die Mädchen heute als kompetenter im Lesen, aber schneiden dafür schlechter in den Naturwissenschaften und in der Mathematik ab als die Jungen.[9] Es sind also weiterhin Geschlechterunterschiede in der Schule erkennbar, weshalb einige Forschende von einer Diskriminierung gegen Mädchen sprechen. Daher beschäftigt sich die folgende Hausarbeit mit der Frage, welche Möglichkeiten zur Prävention und Intervention von Diskriminierung es von Schülerinnen gibt.

---

[1] Vgl. Herwartz-Emden, Leonie/ Schurt, Verena/ Waburg, Wiebke (2012): Mädchen und Jungen in Schule und Unterricht, Stuttgart: Kohlhammer, Stuttgart: Verlag W. Kohlhammer, S.11.
[2] Vgl. Ebd., S.11.
[3] Vgl. Hannover, Bettina/ Ollrogge, Karen et al. 2021.
[4] Vgl. Ebd.
[5] Vgl. Ebd.
[6] Vgl. Ebd.
[7] Vgl. Ebd.
[8] Vgl. Ebd.
[9] Vgl. Ebd.

3

Zu Erst werden die Begriffe *Diskriminierung* und *Stereotyp* erläutert, bevor auf die zugeschriebenen Geschlechterstereotype der Mädchen eingegangen wird. Es folgen die Auswirkungen und die Rolle der Eltern, Lehrkräfte und Peers auf die Stereotype. Danach werden verschiedene Maßnahmen zur Prävention und Intervention vorgestellt. Zum Schluss folgt ein Fazit.

2. Definition *Diskriminierung*

Unter Diskriminierung wird eine Kategorisierung von Personengruppen verstanden, die zu einer Andersbehandlung aufgrund ihrer sozialen Gruppe führt.[10] Die kategorialen Unterschiede zwischen den Personengruppen werden als Rechtfertigung angesehen, um sie zu benachteiligen.[11] Dabei werden durch Ideologien und Normalitätsmodelle soziale Gruppen unterschieden, wodurch diejenigen, welche nicht dem Ideal entsprechen, nicht als gleichwertig und gleichberechtigt angesehen werden.[12] Es handelt sich bei den Normalitätsmodellen allerdings nicht bloß um gedankliche Konstruktionen, sondern um gesellschaftliche Machtverhältnisse und Unterscheidungen.[13] Bei dem angenommenen Normalfall handelt es sich um eine „erwachsene, männliche, physisch und psychisch gesunde(n) Staatsbürger, der zudem kulturell (Sprache, Religion, Herkunft) und im Hinblick auf äußerliche Merkmale (Hautfarbe) der Bevölkerungsmehrheit bzw. der dominanten gesellschaftlichen Gruppe angehört".[14] Als Folge dieser Ungleichheiten zwischen den sozialen Gruppen, werden den diskriminierten Menschen ihre Menschenrechte mehr oder weniger stark vorenthalten.[15]

3. Definition *Stereotyp*

Stereotype dagegen sind „Überzeugungen über Charakteristika, Eigenschaften und Verhaltensweisen von Mitgliedern bestimmter sozialer Gruppen".[16] Hier wird also über eine Gruppe hinweg generalisiert, wobei Unterschiede innerhalb einer Gruppe ignoriert und nur die Gemeinsamkeiten betrachtet werden.[17] Stereotype können sowohl positiv

---

[10] Glock, Sabine/ Kleen, Hannah (2020): Stereotype in der Schule, Wiesbaden: Springer, S.3.
[11] Scherr, Albert (2012): Diskriminierung. Wie Unterschiede und Benachteiligungen gesellschaftlich hergestellt werden, Freiburg: Springer, S.9.
[12] Vgl. Ebd., S.9.
[13] Vgl. Ebd., S.9.
[14] Ebd., S.8.
[15] Vgl. Ebd., S.9.
[16] Glock, Sabine/ Kleen, Hannah (2020): Stereotype in der Schule, Wiesbaden: Springer, S.2.
[17] Vgl. Ebd., S.2.

als auch negativ sein.[18] So werden Frauen beispielsweise als fürsorglicher angesehen als Männer.[19] Dies wäre ein Beispiel für einen positiven Stereotypen. Stereotype können präskriptiv oder deskriptiv sein.[20] Demnach wäre ein Stereotyp präskriptiv, wenn es sich um Annahmen handelt, wie jemand sein sollte.[21] Präskriptive Stereotype sind meistens positiv, wohingegen deskriptive eher negativ sind.[22] Bei deskriptiven Stereotypen handelt es sich um generalisierte Annahmen, die bestimmen, welche Eigenschaften Mitglieder einer sozialen Gruppe besitzen.[23]

In der Forschung werden jedoch auch noch zwei weitere Formen von Stereotypen unterschieden, nämlich *explizite und implizite.*[24] Unter expliziten Stereotypen werden jene verstanden, „die Menschen bewusst aus ihrem Gedächtnis abrufen können, wenn sie nach ihrer Meinung gefragt werden".[25] Implizite Stereotype sind dagegen jene, die den Menschen nicht bewusst sind, aber in bestimmten Situationen im Gedächtnis aktiviert werden.[26] Das bedeutet, dass implizite Stereotype nicht kontrollierbar sind und unbewusst zu negativen Verhaltensweisen wie Diskriminierung und Ausgrenzung führen können.[27]

4. Geschlechterstereotype gegen Mädchen

Mädchen werden eine Vielzahl an Geschlechterstereotypen zugeschrieben, welche sich entweder auf das Äußere, den Charakter oder auf die Schulleistungen beziehen. Diese werden im Folgenden vorgestellt.

4.1 Aussehen

Eines der typischen Geschlechterstereotype gegenüber Mädchen ist, dass ihnen ihr Aussehen sehr wichtig ist, weshalb sie sich schminken, besonders viele Schuhe kaufen und sich figurbetont kleiden.[28] Studien, in denen Jungs einer Grundschule befragt wurden, warum sie kein Mädchen sein wollen, ergaben, dass Schönheit und modische

---

[18] Glock, Sabine/ Kleen, Hannah (2020): Stereotype in der Schule, Wiesbaden: Springer, S.2.
[19] Vgl. Ebd., S.2.
[20] Vgl. Ebd., S.2.
[21] Vgl. Ebd., S.2.
[22] Vgl. Ebd., S.2.
[23] Vgl. Ebd., S.2.
[24] Vgl. Ebd., S.3.
[25] Ebd., S.3.
[26] Vgl. Ebd., S.3.
[27] Vgl. Ebd., S.3.
[28] Vgl. Valtin, Renate/ Kopffleisch, Richard (1985): „Mädchen heulen immer gleich" – Stereotype bei Mädchen und Jungen, in: Valtin, Renate/ Warm, Ute (Hrsg.): Frauen machen Schule. Probleme von Mädchen und Lehrerinnen in der Grundschule, Frankfurt am Main: Arbeitskreis, S.105.

Attribute besonders oft als negative Gründe angegeben wurden.[29] Mädchen würden demnach übermäßig auf ihr Auftreten achten, weshalb sie sich die Nägel lackieren, sich schminken und sich die Haare frisieren.

Bereits in der Grundschule lässt sich feststellen, dass Mädchen sich geschlechtstypisch kleiden, indem sie buntere Anziehsachen und Schmuck tragen.[30] Auffallend ist allerdings auch, dass die meisten Mädchen lange Haare und Haarschmuck tragen, was in der vierten Klasse dann auf fast alle Schülerinnen zutrifft.[31] In der vierten Klasse fangen sich die ersten Mädchen an zu schminken.[32] Achtet man auf die Schulranzen der Mädchen fällt auch dort auf, dass sie in den ersten Grundschulklassen geschlechtertypische Motive auf ihren Ranzen haben.[33]

Erklärungen zu dem geschlechtertypischen Aussehen der Mädchen gibt es mittlerweile einige. Mädchen versuchen nämlich dem Schönheitswahn der Erwachsenen nachzueifern und passen sich daher an die Geschlechterstereotype an.[34] Sie nehmen sich ihre Mütter als Vorbild und neigen dann dazu sich ebenfalls schminken oder figurbetont kleiden zu wollen. Es ist also eine *Inszenierung der Geschlechterzugehörigkeit*, mit denen Mädchen auf den ersten Blick sichtbar machen, dass sie dem weiblichen Geschlecht angehören.[35]

4.2 Charaktereigenschaften

Mit Blick auf die Studie von Valtin, zeigt sich bei den Stereotypen gegenüber Mädchen, dass Jungen sie als überempfindlich, ängstlich und nicht mutig wahrnehmen.[36] Mädchen würden vor allem im Grundschulalter dazu neigen, andere zu verpetzen und bei Problemen sofort anzufangen zu „heulen".[37] Auch Eigenschaften wie eine relative Inkompetenz, Irrationalität, ein geringes moralisches Urteilsvermögen oder Passivität

---

[29] Vgl. Valtin, Renate/ Kopffleisch, Richard (1985): „Mädchen heulen immer gleich" – Stereotype bei Mädchen und Jungen, S.105.
[30] Vgl. Bülow, Sandra (2008): Geschlechterstereotype in der Grundschule. Eine Studie zur Existenz, Variabilität und Konstanz von Stereotypen sowie zur möglichen Einflussgröße Lehrwerk, in: Steins, Gisela: Geschlechterstereotype in der Schule – Realität oder Mythos?, Lengerich: Pabst, S.143.
[31] Vgl. Ebd., S.143.
[32] Vgl. Ebd., S.143.
[33] Vgl. Ebd., S.143.
[34] Vgl. Valtin, Renate (2020): „Warum ich gern ein Mädchen oder ein Junge bin." Selbstbilder und Stereotype von Mädchen und Jungen, S.106.
[35] Vgl. Herwartz-Emden, Leonie/ Schurt, Verena/ Waburg, Wiebke (2012): Mädchen und Jungen in Schule und Unterricht, Stuttgart: Kohlhammer, S.62.
[36] Vgl. Valtin, Renate/ Kopffleisch, Richard (1985): „Mädchen heulen immer gleich", S.105-106.
[37] Vgl. Ebd., S.106.

6

seien demnach „typisch" weiblich.[38] Neben der hohen Anzahl an negativen Charaktereigenschaften, die dem weiblichen Geschlecht zugeschrieben werden, gibt es allerdings auch positive Eigenschaften. Frauen seien demnach fürsorglicher und empathischer als Jungen.[39] Sie hätten zudem ein hohes Interesse am Wohlergehen ihrer Mitmenschen und wünschen sich harmonische Beziehungen.[40]

4.3 Stereotype in der Schule

In der Schule zeigen sich neben den Stereotypen bezüglich des Aussehens und der Charaktereigenschaften noch weitere, welche sich teilweise sogar auf die Schulfächer beziehen.

In der Schule werden Schülerinnen im Arbeits- und Lernverhalten Eigenschaften wie eine höhere Kompetenz zum selbstgesteuerten Lernen, eine höhere Selbstdisziplin sowie ein positiveres Arbeitsverhalten zugeschrieben.[41] Sie haben demnach ein besseres Lern- und Sozialverhalten als die Jungen.

Auch beim Lesen werden Mädchen positive Stereotype zugeschrieben, denn Schülerinnen hätten im Lesen eine höhere Kompetenz als Jungen.[42] In Studien konnte bestätigt werden, dass Mädchen tatsächlich eine bessere Lesekompetenz besitzen, wobei es sich dort nur um einen geringen Unterschied zwischen den Geschlechtern handelt.[43] Auffallend war jedoch der Unterschied hinsichtlich der Lesemotivation, denn Mädchen lesen in ihrer Freizeit deutlich häufiger freiwillig Bücher als Jungen.[44] Dies lässt sich allerdings darauf zurückführen, dass Lehrkräfte und Eltern höhere Erwartungen an Mädchen bezüglich des Lesens stellen, sodass sich in den Studien vermutlich die Auswirkungen der Stereotype auf die Mädchen zeigen.[45] Ähnlich wie beim Lesen wird Schülerinnen eine höhere Sprachkompetenz zugesprochen.[46]

Neben den positiven Stereotypen gibt es allerdings eine Vielzahl an negativen Zuschreibungen. So werden Mädchen für inkompetenter in Mathematik, Sport und den Naturwissenschaften gehalten. Dies zeigt sich laut Studien auch in den

---

[38] Vgl. Hilgers, Andrea (1994): Geschlechterstereotype und Unterricht. Zur Verbesserung der Chancengleichheit von Mädchen und Jungen in der Schule, Weinheim: Beltz Verlag Verlag, S.79.
[39] Vgl. Ebd., S.79.
[40] Vgl. Doering, Bettina (2014): Gute Mädchen – Böse Jungen? Die Bedeutung von Moral für die Erklärung von Geschlechterunterschieden bei delinquentem Verhalten, S.238.
[41] Vgl. Hannover, Bettina/ Ollrogge, Karen et al. 2021.
[42] Vgl. Herwartz-Emden, Leonie/ Schurt, Verena/ Waburg, Wiebke (2012): Mädchen und Jungen in Schule und Unterricht, Stuttgart: Kohlhammer, S.33.
[43] Vgl. Ebd., S.33.
[44] Vgl. Ebd., S.33.
[45] Vgl. Glock, Sabine/ Kleen, Hannah (2020): Stereotype in der Schule, Wiesbaden: Springer, S.88.
[46] Vgl. Hannover, Bettina/ Ollrogge, Karen et al. 2021.

Mathematiknoten, in denen Schülerinnen schlechter bewertet werden.[47] Allerdings schneiden Mädchen in mathematischen Kompetenztests oft auch schlechter ab als die Jungen, was sich auf eine Stereotypendrohung zurückführen lässt.[48] Das bedeutet, „Menschen, die zu einer Gruppe gehören, über die ein negatives leistungsbezogenes Stereotyp existiert, sind in Leistungssituationen mental durch die Vorstellung belastet, das Stereotyp selbst bestätigen zu können."[49]

5. Auswirkungen der Geschlechterstereotype

Die Auswirkungen der Geschlechterstereotype sind drastischer als man vermuten würde. Besonders die negativen Stereotype können zu einer Verringerung des Selbstwertgefühls und des Selbstbewusstseins führen.[50] Dies kann bei Mädchen und jungen Frauen die psychische Gesundheit beeinflussen und zu einer geringeren psychischen Stabilität führen.[51] Außerdem neigen Mädchen dazu, sich die „weiblichen" Attribute anzueignen, damit sie die Stereotype erfüllen und von der Gesellschaft ohne Probleme akzeptiert werden.[52] Schülerinnen neigen dazu ihre psycho-soziale Überforderung mit der Anpassung an die Geschlechterstereotype in Form von psychischen Beschwerden auszudrücken, was sich verstärkt in Essstörungen bei jungen Mädchen äußert.[53] Die Essstörung ist demnach ein Versuch aus der klassischen Frauenrolle auszubrechen und ein Hilferuf, dass Mädchen mit der Rollenzuordnung überfordert und unzufrieden sind. Problematisch an den Stereotypen ist vor allem, dass Mädchen keine andere Möglichkeit haben als sich anzupassen. Denn die Peergroup, welche in der Schule die wichtigste Sozialisiationsinstanz darstellt, zeigt wenig Toleranz gegenüber Mitschülerinnen, die sich nicht anpassen wollen und die von der gesellschaftlichen Norm abweichen.[54] Stereotype beeinflussen also die Beziehung zwischen Kindern und Jugendlichen. Studien zeigen allerdings auch, dass Mädchen deutlich stärker unter den Geschlechterstereotypen leiden und sich dies auf die

---

[47] Vgl. Glock, Sabine; Kleen, Hannah (2020): Stereotype in der Schule. Wiesbaden: Springer, S.72.
[48] Vgl. Hannover, Bettina/ Ollrogge, Karen et al. 2021.
[49] Hannover, Bettina/ Ollrogge, Karen et al. 2021.
[50] Vgl. Hilgers, Andrea (1994): Geschlechterstereotype und Unterricht. Zur Verbesserung der Chancengleichheit von Mädchen und Jungen in der Schule, Weinheim: Beltz Verlag Verlag, S.79.
[51] Vgl. Ebd., S.79.
[52] Vgl. Ebd., S.79.
[53] Vgl. Buddeberg-Fischer, Barbara (1997): Ess-Störungen als Übersteigerung und In-Frage-Stellung des gegenwärtigen weiblichen Schönheitsideals, Zürich: Verlag Rüegger, S.77.
[54] Vgl. Glock, Sabine; Kleen, Hannah (2020): Stereotype in der Schule, Wiesbaden: Springer, S.89.

Persönlichkeitsentwicklung auswirkt.[55] Mädchen sind demnach durch die Stereotype unzufriedener mit sich und ihrem Aussehen, weil sie versuchen sich dem gesellschaftlichen Schönheitsideal anzupassen, was ihnen die Erwachsenen vorleben.[56] Daher fangen Mädchen schon früh an sich zu schminken.

Im Allgemeinen werden Mädchen deutlich mehr negative Stereotype zugeschrieben als Jungen, was dazu führt, dass sie weniger Vertrauen in ihre Leistungsfähigkeit haben und ihre Erfolgsaussichten deutlich geringer einschätzen.[57] Geschlechterstereotype führen letztendlich dazu, dass sowohl Mädchen als auch Jungen ihre Potenziale nicht ausschöpfen, weil sie sich nur das zutrauen, was andere von ihnen erwarten.[58] Dies lässt sich sowohl auf den schulischen Kontext als auch auf den beruflichen Werdegang von Mädchen und jungen Frauen übertragen. Bis heute wählen immer noch viele junge Frauen geschlechterstereotypisierte Berufe aus, in denen sie nur geringe Aufstiegschancen haben.[59]

6. Rolle der Eltern auf Stereotype

Die Eltern sind die engsten Bezugspersonen für ihre Kinder, weshalb sie eine besonders wichtige Rolle bei der Stereotypenbildung einnehmen. Sie fundieren zum Einen als Vorbild für ihre Kinder und sind zum Anderen die wichtigste Sozialisationsinstanz bevor diese die Schule besuchen.[60] Außerdem teilen Eltern ihre Erwartungen und Meinungen mit den Kindern, wodurch sie diese selber aufnehmen. Studien zeigen, dass Eltern ihren Söhnen eine deutlich höhere mathematische Kompetenz anrechnen als ihren Töchtern, aber umgekehrt die Töchter für sprachlich kompetenter halten.[61] Zwar schätzen Eltern ihre Töchter in Mathe schlechter ein als ihre Söhne, trotzdem zeigen sich in Studien keine Unterschiede bei den Noten in Mathematik.[62] Als Folge dieser Stereotype zeigt sich, dass sich die Selbstwahrnehmung der Kinder fachlich unterscheidet und sich die Kinder besonders für die Fächer motivieren können, in denen ihre Eltern sie für besonders kompetent halten.[63] Schätzt man nämlich die eigene

---

[55] Vgl. Valtin, Renate (2020): „Warum ich gern ein Mädchen oder ein Junge bin." Selbstbilder und Stereotype von Mädchen und Jungen, S.106.
[56] Vgl. Ebd., S.106.
[57] Vgl. Ebd., S.106.
[58] Vgl. Hannover, Bettina/ Ollrogge, Karen et al. 2021.
[59] Vgl. Valtin, Renate (2020): „Warum ich gern ein Mädchen oder ein Junge bin." Selbstbilder und Stereotype von Mädchen und Jungen, S.106.
[60] Vgl. Glock, Sabine; Kleen, Hannah (2020): Stereotype in der Schule, Wiesbaden: Springer, S.86.
[61] Vgl. Hannover, Bettina/ Ollrogge, Karen et al. 2021.
[62] Glock, Sabine; Kleen, Hannah (2020): Stereotype in der Schule, Wiesbaden: Springer, S.86.
[63] Vgl. Hannover, Bettina/ Ollrogge, Karen et al. 2021.

Kompetenz in einem Fach für hoch ein, steigt auch die Motivation sich mit dem Fach auseinanderzusetzen erheblich.[64] Dies führt wiederrum auch zu einer besseren Kompetenz in dem Bereich.

7. Rolle der Lehrkräfte auf Stereotype

Ebenso wie die Eltern spielen auch die Lehrkräfte eine große Rolle im Leben der SchülerInnen. Schließlich haben SchülerInnen ihre Lehrkräfte oft mehrfach die Woche im Unterricht und dies für einen langen Zeitraum bis hin zu mehreren Jahren. Dementsprechend macht es Sinn, dass die Lehrkräfte einen großen Einfluss auf die Entwicklung von Stereotypen und die Entwicklung der SchülerInnen haben.[65] Positiv stereotypisierte SchülerInnen erhalten von der Lehrperson oftmals mehr positive Bestätigung und eine höhere Förderung, sodass sich das auf akademische Merkmale der Betroffenen auswirken kann.[66] Bei vielen Lehrkräften fällt allerdings auch auf, dass sie geschlechtsspezifische Erwartungen besitzen, wie zum Beispiel eine höhere Erwartung der Lesefähigkeiten bei Mädchen.[67] Diese Erwartungen haben Auswirkungen auf die Schulleistungen und die akademischen Merkmale von Schülerinnen.[68] Ähnlich wie bei den Erwartungen der Eltern, werden auch das Selbstkonzept und die Motivation der Mädchen von den LehrerInnen beeinflusst.[69] Die schulischen Geschlechterunterschiede werden daher von den Lehrkräften verstärkt und führen dazu, dass sich die Mädchen an die Erwartungen anpassen.[70]

8. Rolle der Peers auf Stereotype

Neben den Eltern und den Lehrkräften spielt auch die Gruppe der Gleichaltrigen eine große Rolle in der Identitätsentwicklung von SchülerInnen.[71] Die Schule ist nämlich nicht nur ein Ort zum Lernen, sondern auch ein Ort der Identitätsentwicklung und Selbstfindung.[72] Alle Klassenmitglieder bringen dabei ihre eigenen stereotypisierten Erwartungen von zuhause mit, wodurch alle SchülerInnen diesen in der Schule ausgesetzt sind. Die Stereotype können dann dazu führen, dass sich die Kinder und

---

[64] Vgl. Hannover, Bettina/ Ollrogge, Karen et al. 2021.
[65] Vgl. Glock, Sabine/ Kleen, Hannah (2020): Stereotype in der Schule, Wiesbaden: Springer, S.88.
[66] Vgl. Ebd., S.88.
[67] Vgl. Ebd., S.88.
[68] Vgl. Ebd., S.88.
[69] Vgl. Ebd., S.88.
[70] Vgl. Ebd., S.88.
[71] Vgl. Ebd., S.88.
[72] Vgl. Ebd., S.89.

Jugendlichen versuchen in der Schule anzupassen, damit sie nicht aus der Klassengemeinschaft und dem Freundeskreis ausgeschlossen werden.[73] Mitschülerinnen, welche nämlich von der Norm abweichen und sich nicht anpassen, werden verachtet, gehänselt und ausgeschlossen.[74] Die Schülerinnen haben also gar keine andere Möglichkeit als die Geschlechterstereotypen anzunehmen, damit sie in der Klasse akzeptiert werden.[75]

9. Prävention und Intervention

Geschlechterstereotype sind seit Jahren ein wichtiges Thema in der Schulpolitik. Dementsprechend viele Möglichkeiten gibt es mittlerweile um gegen eine Diskriminierung von Mädchen aufgrund ihres Geschlechts in der Schule vorzugehen. Einige der Maßnahmen werden nun im Folgenden vorgestellt. Hierzu muss allerdings noch gesagt werden, dass sich einige Präventions- und Interventionsmaßnahmen nicht nur auf Stereotype von Mädchen anwenden lassen, sondern diese ebenso gut bei den Geschlechterstereotypen von Jungen verwendet werden können. Es ist auch wichtig zu betonen, dass gendersensible Fördermaßnahmen sich in keinem Fall nur auf ein Geschlecht beziehen dürfen, denn dann besteht die Gefahr, dass sich Stereotype verhärten und es zu einer weiteren Diskriminierung kommt.[76]

9.1 Sensibilisierung der Lehrkräfte

Eine der wichtigsten Maßnahmen um Geschlechterstereotype entgegenzuwirken, stellt die Sensibilisierung von Lehrkräften dar. LehrerInnen haben eine Vorbildfunktion gegenüber ihren Lernenden, welche ihnen bewusst sein muss. Dementsprechend ist die Entwicklung eines Bewusstseins für ihr Vorbildverhalten hinsichtlich der Identitätsentwicklung ihrer SchülerInnen besonders wichtig.[77] Lehrenden muss daher klar sein, dass sie massiv zu einer Geschlechtergerechtigkeit beitragen können, indem sie „individuelle Interessen und Kompetenzen von Mädchen und Jungen erkennen und dort fördern, wo diese mit Geschlechterstereotypen inkonsistent sind".[78] Vor allem aber müssen Lehrkräfte wissen, dass es Unterschiede in der Lernmotivation, der

---

[73] Vgl. Glock, Sabine/ Kleen, Hannah (2020): Stereotype in der Schule, Wiesbaden: Springer, S.89.
[74] Vgl. Ebd., S.89.
[75] Vgl. Ebd., S.89.
[76] Vgl. Herwartz-Emden, Leonie/ Schurt, Verena/ Waburg, Wiebke (2012): Mädchen und Jungen in Schule und Unterricht, Stuttgart: Kohlhammer, S.91.
[77] Vgl. https://www.kmk.org/fileadmin/Dateien/veroeffentlichungen_beschluesse/2016/2016_10_06-Geschlechtersensible-schulische_Bildung.pdf (Abruf am 12.02.2023), S.8.
[78] Hannover, Bettina/ Ollrogge, Karen et al. 2021.

Selbsteinschätzung und der Kompetenz von Jungen und Mädchen gibt, sodass gar nicht erst eine fachspezifische Diskriminierung bei der Notenvergabe entstehen kann.[79] Sie sollten sich auch immer wieder fragen, ob ihr Denken von Geschlechtsstereotypen betroffen ist und sich dies dadurch bewusst machen.[80] Dies können sie allerdings nur kontrollieren, wenn ihr Denken und Handeln von expliziten Stereotypen gesteuert werden. Ebenso sollten sich Lehrkräfte immer wieder im Unterricht fragen, warum sie bestimmte Entscheidungen getroffen haben.[81] „Fühlen sich die Mädchen z.B. benachteiligt, wenn ich den einzigen Jungen, der sich regelmäßig meldet, öfter dran nehme, als die einzelnen Mädchen, dann hilft es zu erklären, dass ich möchte, dass sich auch die Jungen am Unterricht beteiligen."[82] So verstehen die Lernenden, wie die Lehrkraft ihre Entscheidungen trifft und fühlen sich nicht unfair behandelt.

Im Unterricht muss also eine geschlechtergerechte Pädagogik vorliegen, damit eine Diskriminierung aufgrund von Geschlechterstereotypen verhindert werden kann. Um eine geschlechtergerechte Pädagogik im Unterricht zu erreichen, müssen folgende Punkte von der Lehrkraft beachtet werden:

„1. Gleiche Chancen, Rechte und Möglichkeiten für Jungen und Mädchen

2. Ausgleich, Gleichberechtigung, Abbau von Stereotypen

3. Berücksichtigung individueller Interessen und Lernstrategien

4. Gezielte Förderung in „schwächeren" Fächern

5. Blick auf die Vielfalt unter Jungen und Mädchen

6. Optimierung der Entwicklungspotenziale beider Geschlechter"[83]

In der Kultusministerkonferenz 2016 wurde zudem beschlossen, dass angehende Lehrkräfte bereits im Studium eine Genderkompetenz entwickeln sollen und diese eine wesentliche Qualifikationsanforderung an den Beruf stellen soll.[84] Die Genderkompetenz ist allerdings keine Fähigkeit, welche die Lehrkräfte intuitiv besitzen,

---

[79] Vgl. Hannover, Bettina/ Ollrogge, Karen et al. 2021.

[80] Vgl. Ebd.

[81] Vgl. Jantz, Olaf/ Brandes, Susanne (2006): Geschlechtsbezogene Pädagogik an Grundschulen. Basiswissen und Modelle zur Förderung sozialer Kompetenzen bei Jungen und Mädchen, Wiesbaden: Verlag für Sozialwissenschaften, S.167.

[82] Vgl. Ebd., S.167.

[83] Vgl. Herwartz-Emden, Leonie/ Schurt, Verena/ Waburg, Wiebke (2012): Mädchen und Jungen in Schule und Unterricht, Stuttgart: Kohlhammer, Stuttgart: Kohlhammer, S.86.

[84] Vgl. https://www.kmk.org/fileadmin/Dateien/veroeffentlichungen_beschluesse/2016/2016_10_06-Geschlechtersensible-schulische_Bildung.pdf (Abruf am 12.02.2023), S.5.

denn diese muss erst entwickelt werden.[85] Genderkompetente Lehrende zeichnet aus, dass sie SchülerInnen personenorientiert fördern können, weil sie über eine hohe Sensibilität und Selbstreflexivität verfügen.[86] Lehrkräfte sind sich den Geschlechterstereotypen bewusst und können „im konkreten Handeln entdramatisierend (zu) agieren".[87] Universitäten und Hochschulen haben dabei die Aufgabe die Geschlechtergleichstellung bereits im Studium zu thematisieren und somit zu einer frühen Sensibilisierung bei den Studierenden beizutragen.[88] Auch im späteren Berufsleben sollen Lehrende die Möglichkeit bekommen Fortbildungen zu besuchen, um eine geschlechtersensible Didaktik zu lernen.[89]

9.2 Sensibilisierung der Lernenden

Ähnlich wie bei den Lehrkräften ist es wichtig die SchülerInnen zu sensibilisieren und auch bei ihnen eine Genderkompetenz zu entwickeln.[90] Das bedeutet, dass die Lernenden über Stereotype und deren strukturellen Benachteiligungen Bescheid wissen müssen, sodass sie angemessen und sicher Eingreifen können.[91] Außerdem sollten SchülerInnen wissen, wie sie angemessen in Konfliktsituationen zu reagieren haben und somit über eine ausgeprägte Gesprächskompetenz verfügen.[92] Um dies zu erreichen, können Workshops in Projektwochen angeboten oder Themen wie Stereotype in den Unterricht integriert werden.

9.3 Förderung der Naturwissenschaften

Besonders die MINT-Fächer werden von Mädchen weiterhin gemieden und sind mit Stereotypen belastet, denn gerade in diesen Unterrichtsfächern seien Jungen kompetenter als Mädchen.[93] Biologie ist dabei das einzige Fach in den Naturwissenschaften, welches Mädchen Spaß macht und somit nicht gemieden wird.[94] Um eine Diskriminierung im Bereich der Naturwissenschaften zu meiden, ist es wichtig

---

[85] Vgl. Herwartz-Emden, Leonie/ Schurt, Verena/ Waburg, Wiebke (2012): Mädchen und Jungen in Schule und Unterricht, Stuttgart: Kohlhammer, S.86.
[86] Vgl. Ebd., S.86.
[87] Vgl. Ebd., S.88.
[88] Vgl. https://www.kmk.org/fileadmin/Dateien/veroeffentlichungen_beschluesse/2016/2016_10_06-Geschlechtersensible-schulische_Bildung.pdf (Abruf am 12.02.2023), S.5.
[89] Vgl. Ebd., S.5.
[90] Vgl. Herwartz-Emden, Leonie/ Schurt, Verena/ Waburg, Wiebke (2012): Mädchen und Jungen in Schule und Unterricht, Stuttgart: Kohlhammer, S.88.
[91] Vgl. Ebd., S.89.
[92] Vgl. Ebd., S.89.
[93] Vgl. Matzner, Michael/ Wyrobnik, Irit (2010): Handbuch Mädchen-Pädagogik, Weinheim: Beltz Verlag, S.242.
[94] Vgl. Ebd., S.242.

das Interesse der Mädchen in den Fächern zu erreichen, sie zu fördern und vor allem ihre Selbstwirksamkeitserwartung zu steigern.

Der Psychologe Albert Bandura hat ein Konzept zur Steigerung der Selbstwirksamkeitserwartungen entwickelt, welches sich gut auf die Förderung der Naturwissenschaften anwenden lässt.[95] Bandura geht davon aus, dass vier Punkte angewendet werden müssten, damit die Selbstwirksamkeitserwartungen gesteigert werden könnten. Diese wären: Vermittlung von Erfolgserlebnissen; Lernen am Modell; Suggestion, Zuspruch, Ermutigung; positives Klassenklima.[96] Das bedeutet also, dass Mädchen eine höhere Selbstwirksamkeit erlangen, wenn sie Erfolg erleben und selber am Unterricht teilnehmen können. Das Bundesland Niedersachsen hat sich Banduras Konzept zum Vorbild gemacht und erste Modellversuche wie „Technik zum Be-Greifen speziell für junge Frauen" sowie „Motivation von Frauen und Mädchen für ein Ingenieurstudium" erstellt.[97]

Das Konzept von Bandura lässt sich gut in den naturwissenschaftlichen Unterricht integrieren, indem beispielsweise die Klasse per Zufallsprinzip in Mädchen- und Jungengruppen eingeteilt wird. In koedukativen Gruppen neigen Mädchen dazu bei Experimenten eher zu beobachten und das Protokoll zu führen, sodass keine Steigerung der Selbstwirksamkeitserwartung möglich ist.[98] In „monoedukativen Gruppen „vergessen" Mädchen zeitweise, dass sie Mädchen sind und sind deshalb dem maskulin konnotierten Unterricht aufgeschlossener als in gemischten Gruppen."[99] Sie sind gezwungen alles selbst zu machen und beziehen die Erfolgserlebnisse auf sich selbst. Daher zeigen Studien, dass monoedukative Gruppen in Physik und Chemie zu mehr Spaß bei Mädchen führen und sie sich deutlich mehr zutrauen.[100] Mädchen neigen außerdem dazu genauer zu arbeiten als Jungen, weshalb sie gründlicher und sorgsamer in Experimenten vorgehen.[101]

Lehrkräfte sollten zudem Mädchen ermutigen einen MINT-Schwerpunkt zu wählen, entweder als Leistungsfach oder sogar als mathematisch-naturwissenschaftliches Profil im Abitur.[102] Aber auch die Ermutigung zu Wettbewerben in den Naturwissenschaften

---

[95] Vgl. Matzner, Michael/ Wyrobnik, Irit (2010): Handbuch Mädchen-Pädagogik, Weinheim: Beltz Verlag, S.249.
[96] Vgl. Ebd., S.249.
[97] Vgl. Ebd., S.249.
[98] Vgl. Ebd., S.249.
[99] Ebd., S.250.
[100] Vgl. Ebd., S.249.
[101] Vgl. Ebd., S.249.
[102] Vgl. Ebd., S.252.

kann das Interesse der Mädchen und ihre Motivation erhöhen. Wettbewerbe wie „Jugend forscht", „Chemieolympiade" oder „Schüler experimentieren" existieren bereits und können zur Prävention der Diskriminierung beitragen.[103] Mädchen sollten aber auch in den Naturwissenschaften ermutigt werden an den Schnupperstudientagen an Universitäten im Bereich MINT teilzunehmen.[104]

FachlehrerInnen sollten im Unterricht außerdem darauf achten, dass Naturwissenschaftlerinnen wie beispielsweise Lise Meitner oder Marie Curie thematisiert werden, damit Mädchen sehen, dass auch Frauen in der Forschung große Erfolge erzielt haben.[105] Ebenso ist es ratsam, dass sich die Schulbücherei Werke wie „Chemikerinnen – es gab und es gibt sie" vom Arbeitskreis Chancengleichheit in der Chemie anschafft, um Mädchen zu motivieren.[106]

Um das Interesse der Mädchen in den Naturwissenschaften zu wecken, bietet es sich außerdem auch an Unterrichtsmaterialien an die Interessenbereiche der Schülerinnen anzupassen, wie beispielsweise Aufgaben zum Thema des menschlichen Körpers oder zur Umwelt.[107] Der Alltagskontext und die Lebenswirklichkeit von Mädchen sollten für den naturwissenschaftlichen Unterricht beachtet werden.[108] Eine Beispielfrage zum Thema „Gefahren von Strom" wäre laut Roßberger und Hartinger folgende: „Wo lauern zu Hause und in der Schule Gefahren von Strom?"[109] Die Aufgaben sollten für Mädchen also so lebensnah wie möglich formuliert werden, damit sie sich darunter etwas vorstellen und ihre Gesprächsbereitschaft gefördert werden können.

9.4 Förderung in Mathematik

Frauen werden auch heute noch eher Biologinnen als Mathematikerinnen, was daran liegt, dass sie empathischer sind und sie diese Charaktereigenschaft in der Mathematik nicht brauchen.[110] Genau das ist allerdings auch der Punkt, an dem Lehrkräfte ansetzen können, um das mathematische Interesse der Schülerinnen zu wecken. Wie in den Naturwissenschaften können lebensnahe Aufgaben mit den Themen „Umwelt,

---

[103] Vgl. Matzner, Michael/ Wyrobnik, Irit (2010): Handbuch Mädchen-Pädagogik, Weinheim: Beltz Verlag, S.250.
[104] Vgl. Ebd., S.250.
[105] Vgl. Ebd., S.250.
[106] Vgl. Ebd., S.250.
[107] Vgl. Glock, Sabine/ Kleen, Hannah (2020): Stereotype in der Schule, Wiesbaden, S.90.
[108] Vgl. Von Maltzahn, Katharina (2014): Mädchen und Naturwissenschaften. Zur Entwicklung von Interessen nach der Grundschule, Weinheim: Beltz Verlag, S.123.
[109] Roßberger, Eva/ Hartinger, Andreas (2000): Interessen an Technik. Geschlechtunterschiede in der Grundschule. In: Grundschule 32, H.6.
[110] Vgl. Matzner, Michael/ Wyrobnik, Irit (2010): Handbuch Mädchen-Pädagogik, Weinheim: Beltz Verlag, S.227.

Nachhaltigkeit und Natur" dazu führen, dass Schülerinnen Mathematik positiver wahrnehmen und eine höhere Motivation aufweisen.[111] Aber auch hier ist es sinnvoll Mädchen für Wettbewerbe wie den „Bundeswettbewerb Mathematik" zu ermutigen.[112] Lehrkräfte können ihren Unterricht allerdings auch an das Konzept des dialogischen Mathematikunterrichts anpassen.[113] Dabei sollen Lernende Hefte oder Lerntagebücher erstellen, in die sie „Gedanken und persönliche Bezüge zu einer vorher von der Lehrperson gestellten oder im Unterricht gemeinsam entwickelten möglichst provokanten Kernidee" notieren.[114] Die Lernenden setzen sich schriftlich mit der Kernidee auseinander, wodurch beim Schreiben Gefühle reflektiert und Gedanken verlangsamt werden sollen.[115] In Untersuchungen von Almut Zwölfer zeigte sich, dass der dialogische Mathematikunterricht bei Mädchen zu mehr Begeisterung führte, weil sie das Fach als kreativer wahrnahmen und dadurch eine Motivation aufwiesen.[116]

Da Mädchen allerdings schon von ihren Eltern als inkompetenter als Jungen in Mathematik gehalten werden, sollten Lehrkräfte das mathematische Selbstkonzept der Mädchen fördern. Die allerwichtigste Maßnahme um Schülerinnen in Mathematik zu fördern ist es daher, sie ernst zu nehmen.[117] Respekt und Anerkennung sind nämlich die Basis um ein positives Selbstkonzept entwickeln zu können.[118]

9.5 Förderung in Technik

Ähnlich wie in den Naturwissenschaften und der Mathematik sollten Mädchen ermutigt werden sich mit Technik auseinanderzusetzen, damit sie Spaß daran bekommen. So bietet es sich an Schülerinnen für die Mädchen-Technik-Tage oder für Technik-Abenteuer-Camps zu begeistern, bei denen sie unter sich Mädchen sind und somit ihre Selbstwerterwartungen steigern können.[119] Zudem gibt es das Projekt „Technopedia" bei den Deutschen Industrie- und Handelskammertagen, wo Unternehmen dazu

---

[111] Vgl. Matzner, Michael/ Wyrobnik, Irit (2010): Handbuch Mädchen-Pädagogik, Weinheim: Beltz Verlag, S.227.
[112] Vgl. Ebd., S.227.
[113] Vgl. Herwartz-Emden, Leonie/ Schurt, Verena/ Waburg, Wiebke (2012): Mädchen und Jungen in Schule und Unterricht, Stuttgart: Kohlhammer, S.99.
[114] Ebd., S.99.
[115] Vgl. Ebd., S.99.
[116] Vgl. Ebd., S.99.
[117] Vgl. Matzner, Michael/ Wyrobnik, Irit (2010): Handbuch Mädchen-Pädagogik, Beltz Verlag: Weinheim, S.231.
[118] Vgl. Ebd., S.231.
[119] Vgl. Ebd., S.250.

motiviert werden sollen, Schulen durch Praxisangebote im Rahmen eines berufsorientierten Unterrichts zu unterstützen.[120]

Das große Problem im Bereich der Technik ist noch immer, dass wenige Schulen dies als Schulfach anbieten und es daher schwierig ist, außerhalb von AGs Technik in den Schulalltag zu integrieren.[121] Außerdem fehlen weibliche Rollenvorbilder, weshalb Mädchen sich weiterhin nicht für das Thema begeistern können.[122]

9.6 Maßnahmen im Sportunterricht

Der Sportunterricht zählt noch immer zu den Unterrichtsfächern, in denen auf Mädchen wenig Rücksicht genommen wird. Typisch weibliche Sportarten, wie Tanzen oder Gymnastik, werden von den Lehrkräften nicht als „richtigen Sport" angesehen, weshalb die Bedürfnisse und Stärken der Schülerinnen weiterhin vernachlässigt werden.[123] Hier ist es ratsam, dass Lehrpersonen sich „mit Rollenklischees im Sportunterricht und den vom Sport verursachten Weiblichkeitszwängen auseinandersetzen".[124] Jungen und Mädchen sollten den Sportunterricht mitgestalten dürfen und ein Mitspracherecht haben. Außerdem nimmt bei Mädchen die Lust am Spielen zu, wenn sie den Sinn hinter der Sportart verstehen, sodass Lehrkräfte dies im Vorherein erklären sollten.[125] Um den Unterricht an die Schülerinnen anzupassen, könnten Lehrkräfte den Sportunterricht durch Musik und Rhythmus begleiten lassen.[126]

Problematisch ist allerdings heute noch immer, dass der Lehrplan die Sportarten vorgibt und Lehrkräfte daher wenig Freiraum haben etwas anderes mit den SchülerInnen im Unterricht zu machen. An dieser Stelle ist es wichtig zu betonen, dass die klassischen Sportarten nicht aus dem Lehrplan gestrichen werden sollten, da sie den Durchsetzungswillen, den Krafteinsatz und den Mut der Mädchen fördern können.[127] Es geht vielmehr darum, dass Sportarten so gewählt werden, dass sich beide Geschlechter in den Unterricht integriert und ernstgenommen fühlen.

---

[120] Vgl. Matzner, Michael/ Wyrobnik, Irit (2010): Handbuch Mädchen-Pädagogik, Beltz Verlag: Weinheim, S.263.
[121] Vgl. Ebd., S.259.
[122] Vgl. Ebd., S.259.
[123] Vgl. Ebd., S.355.
[124] Vgl. Ebd., S.358.
[125] Vgl. Ebd., S.358.
[126] Vgl. Ebd., S.358.
[127] Vgl. Ebd., S.354.

9.7 Girls Day

Der Girls Day, auch Zukunftstag genannt, ist ein Aktionstag, der Mädchen eine gute Möglichkeit bietet, einen Tag in einen anderen Beruf herein zu schnuppern, den sie sich sonst nicht ausgesucht hätten und in dem es nur eine geringe Frauenquote gibt. Hierzu zählen Berufe und Studiengänge der IT, aus dem Handwerk, den Naturwissenschaften und der Technik.[128] Mädchen sollen also einen Tag in einem „typischen" Männerberuf verbringen. Sie „sollen die Möglichkeit bekommen, sich frei nach ihren Talenten und ihren Neigungen für eine Ausbildung oder ein Studium zu entscheiden."[129] Die Mädchen bekommen damit die Chance weiblichen Vorbildern in Führungspositionen aus der Politik oder der Wirtschaft zu begegnen.[130] Beim Girls Day lernen die Mädchen dabei nicht nur einen Beruf kennen, in dem sonst das männliche Geschlecht arbeitet, sondern sammeln auch Erfahrungen und weiten ihren Blick auf möglicherweise spannende Berufsfelder. Da der Girls Day jedes Jahr stattfindet, haben Mädchen die Möglichkeit in ihrer Schullaufbahn mehrfach in unterschiedliche Berufe zu schauen.

In der Schule macht es vorher Sinn den Girls Day vorzubereiten und sich bereits im Vorhinein mit Geschlechterklischees in der Berufswelt, Rollenbildern und unterschiedlichen Lebensentwürfen der Geschlechter auseinanderzusetzen.[131] Evaluationsergebnisse zeigen nämlich, dass Mädchen zufriedener mit dem Aktionstag waren, wenn dieser vor- und nachbereitet wurde.[132]

Der Zukunftstag zeigt allerdings Erfolge, denn die Zahlen in den MINT-Studiengängen steigen und viele Mädchen haben durch den Girls Day ihren Beruf gefunden.[133]

So gut dieses Prinzip auch klingt, es hat seine Tücken. Einige Schülerinnen nutzen den Aktionstag um die Schule schwänzen zu können oder um in einen Beruf hinein zu schnuppern, welcher gar nicht zu den Männerberufen zählt. Daher sollten LehrerInnen die Mädchen bei ihrer Berufswahl vorher beraten oder auch von ausgewählten Berufen abraten, wenn dieser kein „typischer" Männerberuf ist. Im Internet finden sich Listen zu „typischen" Männerberufen, auf welche die Lehrkräfte die Schülerinnen hinweisen könnten.

---

[128]https://mediaserve.kompetenzz.net/filestore/2/6/0/5/2_04f8259cdd5a1f3/26052_7a87a9f990e24d4.pdf?v=1652785254 (Abruf am 12.02.2023), S.3.
[129] https://www.girls-day.de/content/download/358/file/schulbroschuere.pdf (Abruf am 12.02.2023), S.3.
[130] Vgl. Ebd., S.3.
[131] Vgl. Ebd., S.4.
[132] Vgl. Ebd., S.4.
[133] Vgl. Ebd., S.4.

9.8 Kurse zur Präventionsarbeit am Beispiel der Laborschule Bielefeld

Die Laborschule Bielefeld ist eine Reformschule, die sich von dem typischen deutschen Schulsystem abhebt. Hierbei soll nicht näher darauf eingegangen werden, was die Schule so besonders macht. Es ist allerdings wichtig zu wissen, dass die Laborschule Bielefeld das Thema Geschlecht an vielen Stellen in den Schulalltag integriert und sich ein eigenes Konzept dazu entwickelt hat. Unteranderem bietet die Schule verschiedene Themen zur Präventionsarbeit im Bereich der Sexualerziehung an, die jeweils an die Jahrgangsstufen angepasst werden.[134] Dabei werden die SchülerInnen regelmäßig gebeten zu brainstormen, welche Themen sie in der Präventionsarbeit interessieren würden, damit die LehrerInnen neue Ideen entwickeln können. Zwei dieser Themen aus der Präventionsarbeit würden sich auch in den Unterricht von Regelschulen integrieren lassen.

Ein Thema der Präventionsarbeit heißt „Die persönlichen Stärken fordern und fördern".[135] Dabei setzen sich die SchülerInnen mit ihrem Selbstbild auseinander, damit sie im Anschluss an das Projekt ein positiveres Selbstwertgefühl entwickeln können. Die TeilnehmerInnen erstellen eine Collage über sich selbst, in dem sie auf ein Plakat wichtiges aus ihrem Leben schreiben, malen oder herauf kleben. Die Lehrkraft kann den SchülerInnen im Vornherein ein Beispielexemplar zeigen, damit diese eine Idee haben, wie so etwas aussehen könnte. Die Collage fördert nicht nur die Kreativität, sondern lässt die Lernenden über ihre Stärken nachdenken und sich diese bewusst machen.[136] Die Idee der Collage lässt sich allerdings auch abwandeln, denn die SchülerInnen können stattdessen individuell ein lebensgroßes Körperbild ausschneiden und dort die eigenen Stärken und Kompetenzen herausarbeiten.[137]

Ein weiteres mögliches Thema zur Präventionsarbeit wäre „Rollenbilder – Reflexion der Geschlechterrollen und der sozialen Beziehungen".[138] Mädchen und Jungen lernen schon in der Kindheit, dass ihr Handeln je nach Geschlecht von der Gesellschaft unterschiedlich bewertet wird und deswegen ist es wichtig die SchülerInnen zu sensibilisieren. Geschlechterstereotype „beeinflussen weiterhin die Art und Weise, wie sich Mädchen und Jungen schon als Kinder die Welt, insbesondere auch ihren Körper

---

[134] Vgl. Cerulla, Britta/ Schütte, Marlene (2014): Geschlechterbewusste Sexualerziehung und –pädagogik, Bad Heilbrunn: Julius Klinkhardt, S.88.
[135] Vgl. Ebd., S.88.
[136] Vgl. Ebd., S.88.
[137] Vgl. Ebd., S.88.
[138] Vgl. Ebd., S.90.

und ihre Sexualität aneignen."[139] In der Schule lassen sich die Geschlechterrollen noch deutlich beobachten, weswegen dieses Thema besonders wichtig ist. Die Mädchen und Jungen sollen sich anhand von Gedankenspielen die Geschlechterrollen deutlich machen. Methoden für den Unterricht wären: „Typisch Mädchen, typisch Junge", „Wenn ich ein Mädchen/ Junge wäre, müsste ich..." oder „Wenn ich ein Mädchen/ Junge wäre, dürfte ich...".[140] Die Lehrkraft kann dabei selber entscheiden, ob die Mädchen und Jungen dies geschlechtergetrennt, –gemischt oder in Einzel-, Partner- oder Gruppenarbeit bearbeitet werden soll.

Zwar nutzt die Laborschule Bielefeld die Präventionsarbeit nicht im Unterricht, sondern als Kurse für die SchülerInnen, trotzdem könnten solche Themen gut in den Unterricht integriert oder an Projekttagen zum Thema gemacht werden. Dabei könnten Schulen ExpertInnen einladen, welche die Lernenden über Themen wie Körperbilder/ Körperideale, Depressionen oder Mädchensein/ Jungesein informieren.[141]

9.9 Elternbildung

Wie bereits erwähnt, haben Eltern eine wichtige Vorbildfunktion gegenüber ihren Kindern und sind dementsprechend an der Entstehung von Stereotypen beteiligt. Daher kann eine Prävention nicht nur in der Schule stattfinden, sondern muss auch zuhause bei den SchülerInnen weitergeführt werden. Eine geschlechtergerechte Pädagogik in der Schule kann nämlich nur funktionieren, „wenn Kinder und Jugendliche in ihrem individuellen Denken und mit ihren subjektiven Interessen Annahme und Wertschätzung erfahren."[142] Daher muss auch hier angesetzt werden, um eine Diskriminierung von Mädchen in der Schule zu verhindern und die Schülerinnen in ihren Selbsteinschätzungen zu stärken. Eltern muss bewusst gemacht werden, dass ihre elterlichen Erwartungen den Schulerfolg massiv beeinflussen und besonders das mathematische Selbstkonzept ihrer Töchter darunter leidet.[143] Lehrkräfte könnten Elternabende nutzen, um diese über die Auswirkungen der Geschlechterstereotype zu informieren und sie dazu zu bringen ihr eigenes Denken bezüglich der Stereotype zu überdenken.

[139] Cerulla, Britta/ Schütte, Marlene (2014): Geschlechterbewusste Sexualerziehung und –pädagogik, Bad Heilbrunn: Julius Klinkhardt, S.90.
[140] Ebd., S.90.
[141] In Anlehnung an: Biermann, Christine: Mädchenkurse - alte und neue Zielvorstellungen und ihre aktuelle Umsetzung, S.107.
[142] Vgl. Herwartz-Emden, Leonie/ Schurt, Verena/ Waburg, Wiebke (2012): Mädchen und Jungen in Schule und Unterricht, Stuttgart: Kohlhammer, S.90.
[143] Vgl. Glock, Sabine/ Kleen, Hannah (2020): Stereotype in der Schule, Wiesbaden: Springer, S.90.

Eine weitere Möglichkeit wäre es den Tag der offenen Tür in der Schule zu nutzen. Lernende könnte vorher die Geschlechterstereotype und ihre Auswirkungen erarbeiten, welche sie dann in der Schule aushängen oder sogar präsentieren. Lehrkräfte könnten hier aber auch die Beispielthemen der Präventionsarbeit von der Laborschule Bielefeld nutzen, sodass diese den Eltern vorgestellt werden.

9.10 Antidiskriminierungsbeauftragte

„Präventions- und Interventionsmaßnahmen können nur dann nachhaltig funktionieren, wenn sie institutionalisiert werden."[144] Das bedeutet, dass die Schule die Diskriminierung ernst nehmen und ein *gesamtschulisches Antidiskriminierungskonzept* entwickeln muss.[145] Eine Möglichkeit für dieses Konzept wäre es Antidiskriminierungsbeauftrage an Schulen anzustellen.[146] Dabei würde es nicht nur um die Diskriminierung von Mädchen gehen, sondern um alle Formen der Diskriminierung. Antidiskriminierungsbeauftragte wären dann dafür zuständig den Lernenden Hilfestellung und Lösungsvorschläge bei einer geschlechterspezifischen Diskriminierung zu geben. Sie sollten also die Anlaufpersonen sein, wenn sich jemand aufgrund des Geschlechts diskriminiert fühlt.

Schulen hätten dabei die Wahl bereits bestehende Personen der Schule wie VertrauenslehrerInnen oder SozialarbeiterInnen für die Aufgabe weiterzubilden oder jemanden Neues einzustellen.[147] „Weiterhin könnten auch Gremien oder Arbeitsgemeinschaften zum Thema Antidiskriminierung gegründet werden."[148]

Das Bundesland Berlin gilt in dem Bereich als Vorreiter, denn es ist das einzige Bundesland, welches eine Stelle als Antidiskriminierungsbeauftragte geschaffen hat.[149] Um gegen die Diskriminierung vorzugehen hat die Antidiskriminierungsbeauftragte von Berlin beispielsweise eine Fortbildung für die Lehrenden entwickelt.[150]

---

[144] Antidiskriminierungsstelle des Bundes (2019): Diskriminierung an Schulen erkennen und vermeiden. Praxisleitfaden zum Abbau von Diskriminierung in der Schule, S.29.
[145] Vgl. Ebd., S.29.
[146] Vgl. Ebd., S.29.
[147] Vgl. Ebd., S.31.
[148] Vgl. Ebd., S.31.
[149] Vgl. Pürckhauer et al. 2019
[150] Vgl. Ebd.

10. Fazit

Zusammenfassend lässt sich sagen, dass Mädchen besonders in den mathematischen und naturwissenschaftlichen Fächern Diskriminierung durch eine ungerechte Notenvergabe erleben und Lehrende ihnen in vielen Bereichen weniger zutrauen als Jungen. Mädchen können also nicht als „Bildungsgewinnerinnen" betrachtet werden, denn dafür werden sie noch immer in zu vielen Bereichen benachteiligt. Zwar gibt es bereits viele Projekte, wie Mädchen in den naturwissenschaftlichen und mathematischen Bereichen gefördert werden sollen, doch trotzdem beeinflussen Geschlechterstereotype noch immer das Selbstkonzept und die Motivation der Schülerinnen. Die Auswirkungen der Diskriminierung sind massiv, denn sie wirken sich bei Mädchen schnell auf die Psyche aus. Schulen sollten daher neben den bereits bestehenden Projekten und Maßnahmen den Fokus auf die Sensibilisierung der Lehrkräfte, Eltern und MitschülerInnen setzen. Stereotype können nämlich nur vermieden werden, wenn sich die Mitmenschen reflektieren und ihre eigenen Stereotype überdenken. Außerdem sollten Mädchen ihr Selbstkonzept stärken, indem Geschlechterstereotype im Unterricht, in AGs oder Projekttagen thematisiert werden. Bundesländer und Schulen sollten sich auch fragen, was sie präventiv gegen geschlechterspezifische Diskriminierung von Mädchen tun können und sich ein Beispiel an der Laborschule Bielefeld oder dem Bundesland Berlin nehmen.

11. Inhaltsverzeichnis

Antidiskriminierungsstelle des Bundes (2019): Diskriminierung an Schulen erkennen und vermeiden. Praxisleitfaden zum Abbau von Diskriminierung in der Schule, Online unter: https://www.antidiskriminierungsstelle.de/SharedDocs/downloads/DE/publikationen/Le itfaeden/leitfaden_diskriminierung_an_schulen_erkennen_u_vermeiden.pdf?_blob=pu blicationFile&v=4 (Aufruf am 12.02.2023).

Baier, Dirk (2014): Von der „Krise der Jungen" zum „Triumph der Mädchen": Entwicklung der Geschlechterrollenorientierung in Deutschland, in: Mößle, Thomas; Pfeiffer, Christian/ Baier, Dirk: Die Krise der Jungen. Phänomenbeschreibung und Erklärungsansätze, Baden-Baden: Nomos, S.257- 270.

Biermann, Christine (2014): Mädchenkurse – alte und neue Zielvorstellungen und ihre aktuelle Umsetzung, in: Biermann, Christine/ Schütte, Marlene: Geschlechterbewusste Pädagogik an der Laborschule Bielefeld, Bad Heilbrunn: Verlag Julius Klinkhardt, S.99-110.

Buddeberg-Fischer, Barbara (1997): Ess-Störungen als Übersteigerung und In-Frage-Stellung des gegenwärtigen weiblichen Schönheitsideals, in: Lauer, Urs; Rechsteiner, Maya; Ryter, Annamaria: Dem heimlichen Lehrplan auf der Spur. Koedukation und Gleichstellung im Klassenzimmer, Zürich: Verlag Rüegger, S.77-86.

Bülow, Sandra (2008): Geschlechterstereotype in der Grundschule. Eine Studie zur Existenz, Variabilität und Konstanz von Stereotypen sowie zur möglichen Einflussgröße Lehrwerk, in: Steins, Gisela: Geschlechterstereotype in der Schule – Realität oder Mythos?, Lengerich: Pabst.

Cerulla, Britta/ Schütte, Marlene (2014): Geschlechterbewusste Sexualerziehung und – pädagogik, In: Biermann, Christine/ Schütte, Marlene: Geschlechterbewusste Pädagogik an der Laborschule Bielefeld, Bad Heilbrunn: Verlag Julius Klinkhardt, S.81-98.

Doering, Bettina (2014): Gute Mädchen – Böse Jungen? Die Bedeutung von Moral für die Erklärung von Geschlechterunterschieden bei delinquentem Verhalten, in: Mößle, Thomas/ Pfeiffer, Christian/ Baier, Dirk: Die Krise der Jungen. Phänomenbeschreibung und Erklärungsansätze, Baden-Baden: Nomos, S.237-256.

Glock, Sabine/ Kleen, Hannah (2020): Stereotype in der Schule, Wiesbaden: Springer.

Hannover, Bettina/ Ollrogge, Karen (2021): Bildungsungleichheiten zwischen den Geschlechtern, Online unter: https://www.bpb.de/themen/bildung/dossier-bildung/315992/bildungsungleichheiten-zwischen-den-geschlechtern/ (Aufruf am 12.02.2023).

Herwartz-Emden, Leonie/ Schurt, Verena/ Waburg, Wiebke (2012): Mädchen und Jungen in Schule und Unterricht, Stuttgart: Kohlhammer.

Hilgers, Andrea (1994): Geschlechterstereotype und Unterricht. Zur Verbesserung der Chancengleichheit von Mädchen und Jungen in der Schule, Weinheim: Juventa Verlag.

Jantz, Olaf/ Brandes, Susanne (2006): Geschlechtsbezogene Pädagogik an Grundschulen. Basiswissen und Modelle zur Förderung sozialer Kompetenzen bei Jungen und Mädchen, Wiesbaden: Verlag für Sozialwissenschaften.

Kompetenzzentrum Technik-Diversity-Chancengleichheit e. V. (2022): Alles zu den Aktionstagen. Informationen für Lehrkräfte, Online unter: https://mediaserve.kompetenzz.net/filestore/2/6/0/5/2_04f8259cdd5a1f3/26052_7a87a9f990e24d4.pdf?v=1652785254 (Aufruf am 12.02.2023).

Kompetenzzentrum Technik-Diversity-Chancengleichheit e.V.: Schulbroschüre. Informationen & Praxishilfen für Lehrerinnen und Lehrer. Girls Day. Mädchen-Zukunftstag, Online unter: https://www.girls-day.de/content/download/358/file/schulbroschuere.pdf.

Kultusministerkonferenz (2016): Leitlinien zur Sicherung der Chancengleichheit. durch geschlechtersensible schulische Bildung und Erziehung, Online unter: https://www.kmk.org/fileadmin/Dateien/veroeffentlichungen_beschluesse/2016/2016_10_06-Geschlechtersensible-schulische_Bildung.pdf.

Matzner, Michael/ Wyrobnik, Irit (2010): Handbuch Mädchen-Pädagogik, Weinheim: Beltz Verlag.

Pürckhauer, Andrea (2019): Was tun gegen Diskriminierung an Schulen?, Online unter: https://mediendienst-integration.de/artikel/was-tun-gegen-diskriminierung-an-schulen.html. (Aufruf am 12.02.2023).

Roßberger, Eva/ Hartinger, Andreas (2000): Interessen an Technik. Geschlechtsunterschiede in der Grundschule. In: Grundschule 32, H.6, S.15-17.

Scherr, Albert (2012): Diskriminierung. Wie Unterschiede und Benachteiligungen gesellschaftlich hergestellt werden, Freiburg: Springer.

Valtin, Renate/ Kopffleisch, Richard (1985): „Mädchen heulen immer gleich" – Stereotype bei Mädchen und Jungen, in: Valtin, Renate/ Warm, Ute: Frauen machen Schule. Probleme von Mädchen und Lehrerinnen in der Grundschule, Frankfurt am Main: Arbeitskreis, S.101-109.

Valtin, Renate (2020): „Warum ich gern ein Mädchen oder ein Junge bin." Selbstbilder und Stereotype von Mädchen und Jungen, S.102-106, Online unter: https://www.pedocs.de/volltexte/2020/20160/pdf/Valtin_2011_Warum_ich_gern_ein_Maedchen.pdf (Aufruf am 12.02.2023).

Von Maltzahn, Katharina (2014): Mädchen und Naturwissenschaften. Zur Entwicklung von Interessen nach der Grundschule, Weinheim: Beltz Verlag.

Milton Keynes UK
Ingram Content Group UK Ltd.
UKHW042212310723
426074UK00023B/502

The TOMBS of the KINGS

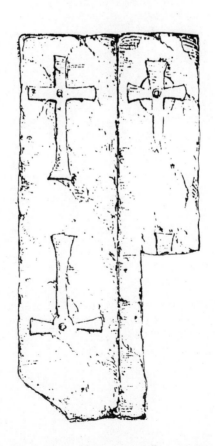

Door in St Oran's Chapel

Illustrations in this book are taken from the *Antiquities of Iona* by H. D. Graham, London, 1850, except for the drawing on page 18 which is from *Sculptured Monuments of Iona & the West Highlands* by James Drummond, Edinburgh, 1881.

THE TOMBS OF THE KINGS

AN IONA BOOK OF THE DEAD

JOHN MARSDEN

First Published in 1994 by
LLANERCH PUBLISHERS, Felinfach
ISBN   1 897853 25 4

The monumental collection of Gaelic hymns and incantations assembled from Hebridean tradition in the last century by Alexander Carmichael and published as his *Carmina Gadelica* includes a *beannachadh buana*, or 'reaping blessing', collected from a crofter on South Uist. Its closing lines form an invocation of Saint Columba - called by his Gaelic name of *Columcille* - which occurs nowhere else in the tradition of the Gael and has its own especial significance for this *Iona Book of the Dead*.

Chalum-chille nam feart 's nan tuam

'Columcille of the graves and tombs'

CONTENTS

Ruiny Cezarea

PREFACE

Few pilgrims to Iona can have approached its hallowed burial-ground in so sceptical a mood as did Dr Samuel Johnson on an October morning in the year 1773. Dr Johnson's travelling companion, James Boswell, describes their visit in his *Journal of a Tour to the Hebrides with Samuel Johnson, LLD.*

> We were both disappointed, when we were shown what are called the monuments of the kings of Scotland, Ireland, and Denmark, and of a King of France.
> There are only some grave-stones flat on the earth, and we could see no inscriptions. How far short was this of marble monuments, like those in Westminster Abbey, which I had imagined here!

Dr Johnson's own account of their Hebridean journey expands on Boswell's observations.

> Iona has long enjoyed, without any very credible attestation, the honour of being reputed the cemetery of the Scottish Kings. It is not unlikely that, when the opinion of local sanctity was prevalent, the Chieftains of the Isles, and perhaps some of the Norwegian or Irish princes were reposited in this venerable enclosure. But by whom the subterraneous vaults are peopled is now utterly unknown. The graves are very numerous, and some of them undoubtedly contain the remains of men, who did not expect to be so soon forgotten.

With every respect to his great learning, the good Doctor was not best-acquainted with the early sources of Scottish history.

The reputation of Iona as the site of the tombs of the kings is a genuinely historical tradition and one which has been taken at its face value by some number of visitors to the island, both before and after Johnson and Boswell. Consequently, it is a tradition deserving of examination in the light of the earliest reliable historical record and such is the first intention of these pages. I have set out to identify the kings whose burial on Iona is confirmed by those early sources of history, and to offer the modern reader some account of each one's life and times that they may not 'be so soon forgotten.'

In so doing, it may be possible to shed some light on the origins of the tradition of Iona as the burial-place of kings and, perhaps also, on the significance of that tradition in the emergence of the Scottish nation.

J.M.

REILIG ODHRAIN

The Burial-ground of Odhran

In the second year after the battle of Culdrevny, and in the forty-second year of his age, Saint Columba sailed from Ireland to Britain. seeking to become a pilgrim for Christ.

Thus Adamnan, the ninth abbot of Iona writing in the last decade of the seventh century, sets down the earliest account of the voyage of the holy man *Columcille* to the Irish settlement of Dalriada, on the west coast of what is now Scotland, in the year 563.

Two years later, Columcille - now better known by his Latin name-form of *Columba* - came to the island off the Ross of Mull thereafter called *I-Columcille*. 'Iona of Columcille', and there founded his church. So much and thus far is history, but the strange story associated with the foundation of Iona in the Irish *Life of Columcille* can only be accounted legend.

Columcille said to his people: 'It is good for us that our roots should go under the ground here.' And he said to them: 'It is permitted to you, that some one of you may go under the clay of this island to consecrate it.'

Odhran rose up readily, and what he said was: 'If you would accept me,' said he, 'I am ready for that.'

'O Odhran,' said Columcille, 'thou shalt have any reward therefore, that is, his prayer shall not be granted to anyone at my grave, unless it is from thee he asks it first.' Then Odhran went to heaven.

Sacrificial burial to mark the foundation of a building is

far from unknown in the mythology of the Irish and Britonic Celt and this legend of 'Odhran laid in earth on I-Columcille' must be interpreted as an archaic survival from pagan Celtic tradition. It would otherwise represent a sinister anachronism in the life of a Christian saint and is anyway, in this case, historically untenable.

Adamnan makes no mention of any Odhran in his *Life of Columba* and neither is the name included among those of 'the twelve men who sailed over with Saint Columba from Ireland' listed as an appendix to the second oldest Adamnan manuscript.

Nonetheless, there was an historical Saint Odhran, identified by the ancient list of holy men preserved in *The Book of Ballymote* as 'Odhran of Iona, of severe piety'. His feast is commemorated on 27th October in the eighth-century *Martyrology of Oengus* and his obituary entered by the Irish *Annals of the Four Masters* at AD 548, fifteen years before Columba sailed from Ireland and seventeen years before his foundation on Iona.

The evidence of so many commemorative Hebridean place-names - among them Kiloran on Colonsay and the island name of nearby Oronsay - firmly associate Odhran with the western seaboard and, most especially, with Iona where the oldest surviving building on the island is 'Saint Oran's Chapel'. The present building with its fine Norman doorway arch is at least a hundred years later than the chapel raised on the same site, and very possibly over the foundations of earlier oratory-shrines with the same dedication, by Queen Margaret of Scotland in 1073.

Beside Odhran's chapel - and some little distance to the south-west of Columba's own shrine beside the restored Abbey - lies the *Reilig Odhrain,* the 'burial-ground of Odhran', where the tombs of the kings form the most ancient graveyard in all Scotland.

10

The earliest sources of the legend of 'Odhran laid in earth on I-Columcille' can be traced back no further than the Irish *Life of Columcille*, which has been dated by the most recent research to the middle of the twelfth century.

The inclusion of the Odhran legend in the Irish *Life* was very probably intended to explain the name of the Reilig Odhrain and to link its dedicatee, however spuriously, with Columba's foundation on Iona. It may well have been in some way associated with the building of the eleventh-century chapel or the enclosure of the burial-ground, because Columba's promise to Odhran – that 'his prayer shall not be granted to anyone at my grave, unless it is from thee he asks it first' – corresponds precisely to the pilgrim's way which passes through the Reilig Odhrain before coming to the site of Columba's shrine at the Abbey. The author of the Irish *Life* was evidently familiar with the course of this 'Street of the Dead' on Iona and, by inference, with the tradition of the Reilig Odhrain as the site of the tombs of the kings.

Neither can it be entirely coincidental that he was writing at much the same time as was the compiler of the Scottish *Chronicle of the Kings*, which includes the most comprehensive and authoritative record of royal interments on Iona. The tradition of the tombs of the kings was already firmly established by the mid-twelfth century, and was not only still current but impressively expanded four hundred years later when Donald Monro, Archdeacon of the Isles, set down his *Description of the Western Isles of Scotland* in 1549.

Within this Isle of Kilmkill there is ane Sanctuary also, or Kirkzaird, called in Erishe *Releag Oran*. In it are three tombs of staine formit like little chapels, with ane braide grey quin stane in the gairle of ilk ane of the tombes. In the staine of ane

is written – *Tumulus Regum Scotiae,* that is, the
Tomb of the Scottes Kings – within this there lay
48 crowned Scottes Kings. The tomb on the south
side has this inscription – *Tumulus Regum
Hiberniae,* that is, the Tomb of the Ireland Kings;
there were four Ireland Kings in it. Upon the
north side of our Scottes tomb the inscription
bears – *Tumulus Regum Norwegiae,* the Tomb of
the Kings of Norway. Within this sanctuary lye
also the maist part of the Lords of the Isles, with
their lynage; twa Clan Leans, with their lynage;
McKinnon and McQuarrie, with their lynage, with
sundrie uther inhabitants of the haille isles.

No king had been buried on Iona for more than
three hundred years by the time of Dean Monro's visit.
Columba's holy island was no longer the royal church
of Scotland's kings, but had been adopted in their stead
by the powerful chieftains of the west, most eminent
amongst them the Lords of the Isles, as their own
dynastic burial-ground. The mystique of the Reilig
Odhrain had thus survived, and even been enhanced by,
the Benedictines who had supplanted the Celtic *culdees*
on Iona in the first years of the thirteenth century.
The patronage of Iona by the clans of Argyll and
the Isles had certainly helped to preserve its tradition
intact through the turbulence of the Reformation on the
evidence of Martin Martin's *Description of the Western
Islands of Scotland,* first published in 1703. His
account of 'St. Ouran's Church, commonly call'd Reliqui
Ouran' includes detailed descriptions of the 'tombs of
the chiefs' but otherwise corresponds almost precisely
to that set down by Dean Monro a hundred and fifty
years before.

On the South-side of the Church is the Burial-place
in which the Kings and Chiefs of Tribes are buried,

and over them a Shrine; and there was an Inscription, giving an account of each particular Tomb, but Time has worn them off. The middlemost had written on it, The Tombs of the Kings of Scotland; of which forty eight lie there.

Upon that on the right hand was written, The Tombs of the Kings of Ireland; of which four were buried here.

And upon that on the left hand was written, The Kings of Norway; of which eight were buried here.

All of which Columba himself would seem to have foretold in his prophetic benediction on Iona, as it was set down by Adamnan within a hundred years of the saint's death.

Small and mean though this place is, yet it shall be held in great and unusual honour, not only by Scotic kings and people, but also by the rulers of foreign and barbarous nations, and by their subjects.

While no historian of early Scotland can afford to totally disregard its contribution, 'tradition' does have a dangerous tendency to perpetuate folklore which cannot be supported by the more reliable historical record and such can certainly be shown to be the case with the tradition of the tombs of the kings.

Two of the four Irish kings are known to have died on Iona in monastic retirement, but there is no evidence for eight kings of Norway having been interred beside them. Even if 'Regum Norwegiae' is taken to mean Norse kings of Man and the Isles, there is some difficulty in firmly identifying any more than half the total of eight. The failure of the earliest reliable sources to confirm the burial of a king on Iona does not, of course, mean that he wasn't buried there. The 'folk-history' of tradition may well preserve evidence which has been lost from the more authoritative historical record, but it may also have been contrived, if not concocted, at a later date and for reasons unconnected to historical scholarship.

Such must be the case with the '48 crowned Scottes Kings' traditionally buried in the Reilig Odhrain. No 'king of Scots' was honoured with that title by the early sources until Malcolm II, who died in 1034. Indeed, the kingdom of the Scots has been historically meaningful only since the mid-ninth century, when the Gaels of the western seaboard and the Picts of the eastern highlands acknowledged the one high-king in the person of Kenneth mac-Alpin.

While Kenneth was not the first royal burial on Iona, the tradition of the tombs of the kings is most firmly focussed on the mac-Alpin dynasty until the end of the eleventh century when Donald III, who was first buried at Dunkeld in 1097 and only later translated to the Reilig Odhrain, became the last king of Scots to be lain in earth on Iona. No more than twenty kings stand between Donald and Kenneth in the Scottish king-lists and some of those are known to have been buried elsewhere than on Iona, so the traditional total of 'forty-eight' kings must fall under immediate suspicion. Nonetheless, the genuine historical record of royal burials on Iona does span more than four hundred years and the roots of the tradition certainly lie much deeper in antiquity than the first emergence of the Scottish nation.

In Scotland, as almost nowhere else, 'the past is a different country'. The land on which Saint Columba first set foot in 563 was one occupied by four different peoples whose forbears had settled its different regions at different points in its prehistory.

The highlands north of the Forth and east of the

Great Glen were commanded, as were the islands from Orkney and Shetland southwards to Skye, by the peoples first identified as *picti* by the Romans in the third century and still called the 'Picts'. They were a fusion of prehistoric aboriginals and a later Celtic overlay into the indomitable warrior stock who had driven the Romans back to the Forth and were still fighting the Northumbrian English on the same frontier in the eighth century AD. They were never more fearsome than when their two principal tribal groupings – the *Maetae* Picts of the southern Highlands and the *Caledonii* Picts of the north – were brought together under a single over-king.

So it was that the centre of Pictish power gravitated to the royal seat of the over-king. In the sixth century it was the hillfort of Craig Phadrig near Inverness where Columba came to seek sanction for his foundation on Iona from the high-king of Picts who had earlier threatened to drive the saint's own people back into the sea. Those people were the original 'Scots', the Gaelic Celts who had been settling the western seabord of Scotland from Ireland since the fifth century. They make their formal entry into early Scottish history when Fergus, Loarn, and Oengus – the 'sons of Erc' and royal heirs to the Irish kingdom of *Dalriada* in Antrim – established themselves in Argyll around AD 500. Oengus on Islay and Loarn at Oban acknowledged the sovereignty of their brother Fergus as over-king and his hillfort at Dunadd in Kintyre as the royal capital to which Columba, himself blood-kin to the house of Erc, came on his arrival from Ireland.

Such, then, were the 'Picts and Scots' who were to form the kernel of the 'kingdom of Scots' in the mid-ninth century, but who had earlier shared the land with two other peoples. The first of these were the Celtic Britons who held the frontier on the Forth-Clyde line in the wake of the departure of the Romans.

The Britonic kingdom of Strathclyde with its royal capital of *Alcluith* on Dumbarton Rock survived as an independent power in the land even until the tenth century when it was finally absorbed into the new Scottish nation. The Britonic kingdom of the *Gododdin* centred on the Firth of Forth was less long-lived than that of their western kindred on the Clyde. By the mid-seventh century, if not earlier, their lands had been claimed by the voracious expansion of the fourth people with territorial claims on what is now called Scotland.

These land-seekers, thrusting north over the Lammermuir hills into Lothian and beyond, were the Germanic warrior-farmers recruited first by the Romans and later by the Romano-Britons as mercenaries settled around Hadrian's Wall. These were the Angles from beyond the Rhine, and their descendants were the northern English whose kingdom of Northumbria expanded through the seventh century until it could claim dominion as far north as the Pictish heartland on the Tay.

The island of Iona is formed of the oldest rock of the earth's crust and was a hallowed place long before the coming of Columba. It was anciently known to the Gael as *I*, *'The* Island', and the same timeless sanctity is echoed in the rune of foretelling preserved in the *Carmina Gadelica* collection of Gaelic lore.

> *Seachd bliadhna roimh 'n bhrath,*
> *Thig muir thar Eirinn ri aon trath,*
> *'S thar Ile ghuirm, ghlais,*
> *Ach snamhaidh I Chaluim chleirich.*

Seven years before the Day of Doom,
The sea shall come over Erin in one watch,
And over blue-green Islay,
But float will Iona of Columba the cleric.

An island formed in the morning of the world and
destined to be the last place destroyed at the world's
end - this was the place held most fitting by the ancient
Celtic peoples for a king to be laid in earth and there to
await the day of doom.

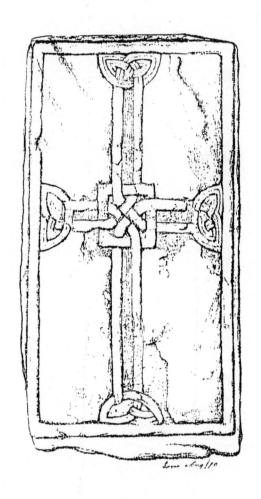

18

THE TOMBS OF THE KINGS

Iom-air o, 'ill-ean mhara,
Iom-air o, 'illean mhara,
'Ill ean o horo eile

Isle of sleep, where dreams are holy,
Sails to thee a king who sleepeth,
With thy saints we leave him sleeping.

Iona Boat Song*

*The *Iona Boat Song* was collected from Hebridean tradition by
Marjorie Kennedy Fraser, the eminent authority on Gaelic music
and song, who died in 1930 and whose ashes are interred in the
Reilig Odhrain.

19

Egfrith, king of Northumbria

In the same year in which king Egfrith had caused this venerable father [Saint Cuthbert] to be ordained bishop [of Lindisfarne], he was killed at Nechtansmere with a great number of the troops which he had taken with him to plunder the land of the Picts.

This happened, as the same father Cuthbert had predicted, upon the thirteenth of the kalends of June [20th May], in the fifteenth year of his reign.

His body was buried in Iona. the island of Columba.

Symeon of Durham,
History of the Church of Durham*

---

* Symeon was one of the nine monks of Durham who opened the coffin of Saint Cuthbert at the translation of 1104 and his *History of the Church of Durham (Historia Dunelmensis Ecclesiae)* was written around that time. It preserves the authoritative historical tradition of the community of Cuthbert through almost five hundred years from the first foundation on Lindisfarne in 635.

Egfrith (OE. *Ecgfrid*) was the last great warrior king of the dynasty founded by Ida at Bamburgh in 547 and he inherited a kingdom at the high peak of its power when he succeeded his father, Oswy, as king of Northumbria in 671.

Oswy's victory over Penda, king of Mercia, in the battle on the *Winwaed* in 655 secured Northumbrian supremacy among the English kingdoms. The *Anglo-Saxon Chronicle* names Oswy as the seventh *bretwalda* – effectively overlord of the Anglo-Saxon kingdoms – and Bede's *Ecclesiastical History of the English People* (c.732) claims Oswy had also 'subdued and made tributary most of the Picts and Irish in the north of Britain'.

The death of Oswy the bretwalda appears to have prompted the Picts to expel the puppet-king imposed on them by Northumbria and rise up against their northern English overlords. So it was that Egfrith's first campaign as warrior-king – and his name translates from the Old English as 'the sword's edge' – took him north in 672 to suppress a Pictish uprising. The closely contemporary *Life* of Egfrith's bishop Wilfrid – who claimed jurisdiction over Pictland as well as Northumbria – tells how the young king 'attacked the vast and invisible forces of the enemy and slaughtered an immense number of their people, filling two rivers with their corpses'.

Two years later, Egfrith was defending his southern frontier against a Mercian-led invasion which he repelled, again with great slaughter, but these military successes of his early reign were not to last. The sheer extent of the Northumbrian imperium was too vast to sustain and Egfrith suffered his first reverse when southern Mercia reclaimed its independence in battle on the Trent in 679. Still more ominous was the threat looming in the north, where a new and ambitious king of the Picts of Fortriu on Tayside was establishing himself as over-king of all the Pictish tribes. Egfrith had followed his father's strategy of conquest of the ancient kingdoms of the north Britons. Just as Oswy had driven out the *Gododdin* to claim the Forth valley for Northumbria, so his son seized the lands of the Britons of *Rheged* in modern Cumbria and north Yorkshire.

Exiled warbands from both Rheged and the Gododdin who had found refuge as mercenaries in Ireland probably prompted Egfrith to launch the raid across the Irish Sea in 684 which 'wasted and destroyed' the plain of Brega, according to the Irish annalist.

The principal beneficiary of these conquests had been the Northumbrian church, and Bishop Wilfrid's foundations at Ripon and Hexham were generously endowed with lands plundered from the Britons. Egfrith's first queen, by a political marriage arranged in his youth, was the chaste East Anglian princess Etheldreda - later Saint Etheldreda of Ely - who encouraged royal land grants and endowments for the great Northumbrian monasteries. When Egfrith married again after Etheldreda's entry into religious life, his second queen, Iurminburg, quarrelled bitterly with Wilfrid who was driven from his see. In 684, Egfrith appointed a reluctant Cuthbert of Lindisfarne to replace the exiled Wilfrid and the following Easter the future Saint Cuthbert was consecrated bishop at York.

Cuthbert had warned Egfrith against renewed war on Pictland, but the threat of a hostile coalition of Pict, Briton and, perhaps also, Dalriadic Scot massing on the northern frontier was too ominous to ignore. By May of the year 685, Egfrith's army had crossed the Forth and was advancing into the Pictish heartland of Tayside. Harassed by guerilla tactics and lured into an ambush east of Forfar, the Northumbrian host was trapped between the hillfort of Dun Nechtain and the swamp of

Nechtansmere. By three in the afternoon of Saturday, 20th May 685, the battle - called *Nechtansmere* by English historians and *Dunnichen* by Scottish sources - was over. Egfrith himself and the greater part of his forces lay dead and the Northumbrian ascendancy which had endured for a hundred years was at an end.

Verses written by the monk Riagal of Bangor in commemoration of the battle - of which he himself may well have been an eye-witness - are preserved in the Irish annals.

> This day the son of Oswy was killed with green
> swords.
> Although he did penance, he shall lie in Hi [Iona]
> after his death...

Egfrith's place of burial is independently confirmed by Symeon of Durham, but neither Symeon nor Riagal explain why a king of the northern English and apparently an oppressor of Pict, Briton and Gael should have been honoured with the first royal interment on Iona to be entered in the early sources of history.

While Egfrith's father Oswy and uncle Oswald had both found sanctuary on Iona during their boyhood exile from Northumbria after the death of their father, King Aethelfrith, in 616, the most likely explanation must lie in Egfrith's blood-kinship to two kings of Picts*. Nennius' *Historia Brittonum* (c.830) describes Bruide**, high-king of Picts and victor in the blood-fray beside Nechtansmere, as Egfrith's *fratuelis* which might best translate as 'first cousin once-removed'. When Oswy and Oswald went into exile on Iona in 616, their elder brother Eanfrith found his way into Pictland

---

* see genealogical chart, p 124
** see p. 25 below.

and there married a Pictish princess. By virtue of the apparent Pictish tradition of matrilinear royal succession, their son Talorcan (d. 657) became a king of Picts. Their daughter, Talorcan's sister, was married to Beli, king of the Strathclyde Britons, and the same right of succession provided Bruide, as the son of that union, with his claim on the kingship of Fortriu and high-kingship of Picts.

Bruide, king of Picts

The body of Bruide, son of Beli, king of the Picts, was brought to Iona, and his death was sorrowful and grievous to Adamnan (abbot of Iona, 679-704), and he desired that the body of Bruide should be brought to him into the house that night. Adamnan watched by the body till morning.

Next day, when the body began to move and open its eyes, a certain devout man came to the door and said: 'If Adamnan's object be to raise the dead, I say he should not do so, for it will be a degradation to every cleric who shall succeed in his place, if he too cannot raise the dead.'

'There is somewhat of right in that,' said Adamnan, 'therefore, as is more proper, let us give our blessing to the body and to the soul of Bruide.'

Thus Bruide resigned his spirit to heaven again, with the blessing of Adamnan and the congregation of Iona.

Life of Adamnan*

* The Irish *Life of Adamnan (Betha Adamnain)* was compiled in the mid-10th century at Kells in Meath, where the community of Iona had found sanctuary from the viking onslaught on the Hebrides some hundred and fifty years earlier.

Bruide, son of Beli and high-king of Picts, must be numbered among the most powerful warlords of the seventh century.

His name is entered in the Pictish king-lists immediately after that of Drust, son of Domnall, whose expulsion in 672 was followed by the uprising so savagely suppressed by Egfrith of Northumbria in the same year. Against that background and for all its legitimation by his mother's Pictish lineage, Bruide's succession to the kingship is best appreciated in terms of *realpolitik*.

He was a son of Beli, son of Neithon and king of the Britons of Strathclyde, and, thus, a prince of the royal house centred on the fortress of *Alcluith* on Dumbarton Rock when the Strathclyde Britons were a great power in the land. His brother Owein, who had succeeded their father as king at Alcluith, slew Domnall Brecc ('Donald the Freckled'), king of Dalriada, in battle at Strathcarron in 642. Whether or not the Dalriadic Scots became tributary to Strathclyde as a consequence, the death of Domnall Brecc certainly heralded the decline of Dalriada through the later seventh century. The kings of Strathclyde were left as the great power in the land with whom the Picts would have sought an alliance after their disastrous defeat of 672. So it must have been that Bruide, son of Beli, came to fill the power vacuum left by Egfrith's wholesale slaughter of the Pictish warrior-aristocracy.

While his first power base was the kingship of the *Maetae,* the southern Picts whose territory south of the Grampians was most vulnerable to Northumbrian expansion, fragments of evidence from the Irish annals*

* All the annals of Ireland are medieval or later compilations from more ancient sources which included a 7th-century chronicle set down on Iona. The *Annals of Ulster* set down in the 15th century and those ascribed to Tigernach of Clonmacnois in the 11th century are considered the most accurate and authoritative.

plot his long campaign to extend his authority from a tribal kingdom centred on Tayside to that of a high-king of all the Pictish tribes from the Ochils to Orkney.

The *Annals of Tigernach* enter 'the destruction of the Orkneys by Bruide' in 682 and the *Annals of Ulster* record a sequence of hillfort-sieges - Dunnottar in the Mearns, Dunadd in Kintyre and Dundurn on Loch Earn amongst them - between 680 and 683, all of which have been interpreted as landmarks in Bruide's phenomenal rise to power. By 685, he had established himself as overlord of Pictland and Dalriada with the claims of kinship to assure him of the support of Strathclyde and he was ready to challenge the Northumbrian dominion beyond the Forth.

It was a challenge which Bruide made good at the battle called by Nennius *gueith linn garann*, 'the fight at the pool of the herons'. Egfrith of Northumbria and the greater part of his forces were slain under the ramparts of Dunnichen Hill beside Nechtansmere in the momentous victory celebrated in the battle-song attributed to Riagal of Bangor.

> This day Bruide fights a battle
>> for the heritage of his grandfather.
> Unless the Son of God wills it otherwise,
>> he will have perished in it ...

> This day [Egfrith] the son of Oswy was killed,
>> who had the black drink.
> Christ has heard our prayers,
>> they spared Bruide the brave.

The Northumbrian frontier had been driven back south of the Forth and no less an authority than Bede was to acknowledge Bruide's triumph as the point from which 'the hopes and strength of the English kingdom began

27

to ebb and slide backwards ...'

For the Picts recovered possession of their own land which the English had held, and the Irish in Britain and also some of the Britons regained their liberty.

There is no record of Bruide's date of birth, but his father had died before 642 and thus he must have been at least middle-aged and probably much older by the time of his death in 693. Neither do the sources hint at his suffering a violent death and so he can be fairly assumed to have died of natural causes at an advanced age. That itself was a remarkable achievement for a warrior king in early Scotland.

Bruide was a friend and contemporary of Adamnan, the abbot of Iona who would have presided over his burial on the island. The *Life of Adamnan* includes an Old Irish elegy for Bruide which is certainly of great antiquity and may even have been the funeral oration composed by Adamnan himself.

Then Adamnan said:
'Many wonders are performed by the King who was born of Mary ... giving death to Bruide, son of Beli.

It is strange that, after he has been king of the north, a hollowed stump of withered oak should enclose the son of the king of Alcluith.'

Niall Frossach, high-king of Ireland

Niall Frossach, son of Fergal, reigned for fifteen years at Tara, according to some of the genealogists; but his reign extended only for seven years before he took religious orders in Iona of Columcille, where he was a monk for eight years; and he died and was buried there.

Dublin Annals of Inisfallen*

.

*   The *Dublin Annals of Inisfallen*, as distinct from the earlier *Annals of Inisfallen*, were compiled - possibly at Inisfallen but certainly in Munster - in the 14th century.

Niall, son of Fergal, owed his cognomen *Frossach*, 'the showery', to the omens attending his birth at Fahan on the Inishowen peninsula and portending his succession as high-king at Tara. Bardic verses celebrating these portents of the 'three showerings' are preserved in the *Annals of Ulster.*

The three showers of Ard-Uilinne,
From heaven [fell] for love of Niall:
A shower of silver, a shower of wheat,
And a shower of honey.

Fergal's son was manly;
With heroes was his calling;
Since he found all to follow him –
Niall Frossach his name.

A hundred pledges from each Province
The hero Niall exacted.
Brave was the noble, who boasted
That he had thrice exacted them.

Celtic Ireland has been described as 'a land where every dun had its king.' It was a society structured on the tribal clan, or *tuath,* each with its own petty king, or *ri,* whose symbol of power was his *dun* or hillfort. Each *ri* acknowledged his regional overlord, a *ruiri* or 'great king', who in turn owed formal allegiance to the *ard ri,* the high-king. The ancient dignity of the *ard ri* is reflected in the survival of his title of 'high-king at Tara' for centuries after the traditional capital stronghold on Tara hill in Meath had been abandoned in the time of Saint Columba.

By the time of Niall Frossach's succession in 763, the high-kingship had long been the exclusive preserve

30

of the *Ui Neill* – the powerful Irish dynasty claiming descent from the fifth-century war lord *Niall Noigiallach*, 'Niall of the Nine Hostages' – passing in turn between its northern and southern branches for over two hundred years.

Niall Frossach's lineage was of the northern Ui Neill and his immediate family had provided an earlier *ard ri* in the person of his brother, the warlike Aed Allán. Aed had inflicted a devastating defeat on the *Ulaid*, the men of Ulster, near Dundalk in 735 and two years later slew a king of the *Laigin*, the men of Leinster, in single combat, before he himself was killed in battle in 743 by Domnall Midi of the southern Ui Neill who became the new high-king of Ireland.

In the year following Domnall's death in 763, the high-kingship passed peacefully to Niall Frossach. The relative tranquillity of his seven-year reign has been attributed to the temporary satisfaction of the territorial ambitions of the Ui Neill and their ascendancy over the Laigin, but must also owe something to Niall's own pacific disposition. His retirement into monastic life in 770 may well have been prompted by the imminent prospect of the renewed strife which erupted in Leinster in the same year.

While the task of restoring order over the rebellious Laigin with fire and sword fell to his successor, Domnall Midi's son Donnchad, Niall Frossach entered the church as a monk on Iona and there lived out the last eight years of his life.

Thus his passing – entered at 778 in the *Annals of Ulster* – was the 'straw death' of a royal monk and while his tomb must certainly be numbered among those of the four Irish kings in the Reilig Odhrain, Niall Frossach cannot be considered to lie in that burial-ground by any ancient right of kings.

Saint Columba had been a prince of the northern Ui Neill and might himself have become high-king had he not chosen to enter the church. It may well have been that association of tribal kinship with its founding saint which prompted Niall to choose Iona as his monastic retreat, but the retirement of the *ard ri* to Iona certainly contributed to its new prestige which was greater under the abbacy of Bresal (abbot of Iona, 772-801) than at any time since before the death of Adamnan in 704.

By the last quarter of the eighth century, Iona had been the royal church of the northern Ui Neill for over two hundred years and could now justly claim the still-greater eminence of a sanctuary for a high-king at Tara.

Artgal, king of Connaught

AD 782   The staff-taking [entry into monastic life] of Artgal, son of Cathal, king of Connaught, and his pilgrimage to Iona in the following year.

AD 791   The death of Artgal, son of Cathal, king of Connaught, in Iona of Columcille.

Annals of Ulster*

---

* see note, p. 26

Artgal, son of Cathal. was born into the royal house of the *Ui Briúin* whose heartland lay between the rivers Shannon and Clare and who had vied with the rival *Ui Fiachrach* for the kingship of the *Connachta*, the men of Connaught, through the seventh and eighth centuries.

With the exception of a brief resurgence of the Ui Fiachrach under Donn Cathad, the reign of Artgal's grandfather, Muiredach Muillethan (d. 702), had effectively put an end to the rival dynasty's claim on the kingdom. Artgal's father had not succeeded to the kingship of Connaught, but both his uncle Indrechtach (d. 723) and his brother Dubinnrecht (d. 768) had reigned before him.

Artgal's immediate predecessor in the kingship had been his kinsman Flaithri (d. 777) whose reign was troubled by the rebellious *Ui Maine* until he defeated them in battle in 775. Despite the Ui Maine – whose territory was bounded by the Shannon, Lough Derg, and the Slieve Aughty mountains – growing restless again on the death of Flaithri, the succession passed peacefully to Artgal in the same year of 777.

This harmony among the men of Connaught was not to outlast the first year of Artgal's reign and the annals record him in battle beside Lough Ree in 778 where he defeated the Ui Maine 'with some slaughter'. Whether or not that blood–fray discouraged Artgal from the way of the warrior, he seems to have had little enthusiasm for active kingship and reigned for only five years before taking monastic orders. The *Annals of Ulster* enter 'the staff-taking of Artgal' *(Bachall Artgaile)* at 782 and record his 'pilgrimage to Iona' in the following year.

So it was that Artgal, son of Cathal, came to live out the last eight years of his life as a monk on Iona. Neither was he the first of his dynasty to end his days in monastic retirement which had become something of

34

a family tradition established over four generations of the Ui Briúin. His uncle Indrechtach had died and been buried at the great monastery of Clonmacnois on the Shannon in 723. Indrechtach's great-uncle Cellach – who had succeeded Muiredach as king of Connaught and, despite his advanced years, defeated a high-king at Tara in the battle of Corran in 704 – had also died the 'straw death' in monastic retirement in the following year.

It would seem to have been only in his choice of Iona for his monastic sanctuary that Artgal had broken with family precedent. The Connachta had an ancient Columban link in that they had fought beside the northern Ui Neill when Columba led them to victory over the high-king Diarmait at the battle of Culdrevny in 561. For all that, the more probable attraction of Iona for Artgal must have been the eminent example of Niall Frossach, the high-king at Tara who had been buried there only five years before Artgal's retirement.

There is a sad irony in the fact that the abbacy of Bresal which had raised Iona to its pinnacle of prestige in the eighth century was to close under the shadow of the sudden eruption of the viking onslaught in the western sea. Norse warbands had established forward bases in Orkney and Shetland and found themselves within striking distance of the Hebrides. Richly-endowed shrines in undefended monasteries whose founding saints had sought the 'deep peace of the running wave' were now at the mercy of the pagan sea-raiders who were to reshape the passage of western Europe through the early medieval centuries.

The *Annals of Ulster* record the 'devastation of all the islands of Britain' at 794 and the *Annals of Inisfallen* enter 'the devastation of Iona of Columcille' in the following year. The vikings struck again in 802, when 'the burning of Iona of Columcille by the heathens' is entered in the *Annals of Ulster*. Plans were laid to transfer the abbot and his community to the greater safety of the Irish mainland, but before they could find sanctuary in their new monastery at Kells in Meath, the 'fury of the northmen' was visited on Iona for a third time. The annals for 806 record 'the community of Iona slain by the heathens, that is, to the number of sixty eight'.

The abbot and what survived of his community transferred to Meath in the following year and thenceafter all the 'abbots of Iona' were in fact based at Kells.

While the Hebrides were effectively relinquished to the northmen, Iona seems never to have been entirely abandoned.

Some form of residual monastic community remained on the island, perhaps as the guardians of the Reilig Odhrain and the shrine of Columba. The abbot Cellach who had built the church at Kells was to resign his abbacy in 814 and – according to the *Dublin Annals of Inisfallen* – 'returned to Iona of Columcille and was buried there'.

In the course of the first four decades of the ninth century the viking onslaught engulfed the western seaboard. The Hebrides became the *Innsegall,* 'the islands of the aliens', and all that is known of the fate of Iona survives in fragmentary entries from the Irish annals. The raids certainly continued and the annalist records the 'red martyrdom' of the monk Blathmac defending Columba's shrine from the northmen in 825, but there is no evidence for any further royal burials on Iona through almost seventy years after Artgal, king of Connaught.

AD 858

Kenneth mac-Alpin, king of Scots

Kenneth, son of Alpin, reigned over the Scots for sixteen years, after destroying the Picts, and he died in Forteviot, and was buried in the island of Iona, where the three sons of Erc were buried.

Chronicle of the Kings*

* The Scottish *Chronicle of the Kings* survives in a number of variant medieval manuscripts. It was first compiled at St Andrews in the reign of William the Lion (king of Scots, 1165–1214), but draws on sources of much greater antiquity and preserves material from nearly-contemporary accounts of the kings of the mac-Alpin dynasty.

Kenneth, son of Alpin (Gael. *Cináed mac Alpin*). is acknowledged by the *Chronicle of Huntingdon* (c.1290) as 'the first of the Scots to gain the kingship of the whole of Alba, which is now called Scotia'. While he was not the first Scot to have been king of Picts and neither was he the first king to have ruled both Picts and Scots. Kenneth is. nonetheless. firmly and justly established as the founding dynast of the Scottish nation.

It had been the high-kingship of Bruide mac-Beli which elevated the kingdom of Fortriu from the stature of a tribal dominion on Tayside to that of the royal centre of Pictland. Thus the sequence of eighth-century 'kings of Fortriu' bearing Gaelic names reflects the steady infiltration of the Pictish east by Dalriadic royal migrants which was to gather momentum in response to the viking invasion of the western seaboard after 800.

Against that background, Kenneth mac-Alpin has been recognized by historians as a 'latecomer from the Gaelic west' and yet one whose dramatic appearance in the king-lists coincided with a crucial point in the history of early Scotland.

Like so many other Dark Age warlords, his origins are obscure. His given name of *Cináed* is believed to have been Pictish and to suggest him as the son of a Pictish mother, but the historicality of his father remains in grave doubt. Kenneth's father is nowhere entered in the ancient annals of Ireland and the Scottish king-lists which claim 'Alpin' as king in Dalriada immediately before his son are suspected of being a later construction intended to legitimate Kenneth's succession. Medieval tradition claims Kenneth's lineage to have been of the *Cenel Gabrain*, the Dalriadic royal house centred on Dunadd, and while he must have had some such initial power base his ancestry can only have lain with a lesser branch of that dynasty. The most impressive, if coincidental, historical evidence links Kenneth's power base with the newly-established Scandinavian presence in ninth-century Scotland.

He had grown to manhood through the turbulent decades when viking raiding was giving way to Scandinavian settlement along the western seaboard and, thus, would have learned his battle-skill on the dangerous frontier-zone of Norse and Gael. The *Annals of Ulster* confirm his alliance with Guthfrith mac-Fergus, a viking chieftain of the Innsegall whose name proclaims his mixed Gaelic-Norse descent, who 'went to Alba to strengthen Dalriada at the request of Kenneth mac-Alpin' in 837. If the same Guthfrith was responsible for the massacre entered by the annalist at 839 when 'the men of Fortriu were slain beyond counting' by the northmen, it was he who opened the way for Kenneth's sudden rise to power. It can have been no accident of history that the slaughter of the Picto-Scottish ruling house in 839 preceded Kenneth's seizure of the kingship of Dalriada in the following year and of Fortriu two years later.

Gerald of Wales' story of the 'black dinner' in which Kenneth murdered Pictish chieftains trapped between feasting-benches may have been a fiction devised by an eleventh-century historian, but it cannot be denied that the earliest sources for Kenneth mac-Alpin are everywhere steeped in blood. The *'Prophecy' of Berchan* - roughly contemporary with the *Chronicle of the Kings* but drawing on independent bardic sources - calls him 'The Slayer' and speaks of the Picts as 'the fierce men of the east deceived by him... after violent deaths, after violent slaughter in Scone of the high shields'.

Whether or not Kenneth eliminated the rivals to the kingdom of Fortriu whose names appear in Pictish king-lists during his years of reign, his imperium was centred on Tayside and seems not to have extended to the Pictish tribes north of the Mounth. Instead, his ambitions were directed south of the Forth and the *Chronicle of the Kings* records his six invasions of Northumbria, his burning of the northern English stronghold at Dunbar, and his seizure of the Northumbrian monastery on the Tweed at Old Melrose.

It would seem that the mac-Alpin dynasty imposed its own Gaelic language and culture on the new kingdom of Alba to such an extent that the history of the Picts came to an end with the reign of Kenneth. Nonetheless, his kingdom was raised over the deep foundations of the 'kingdom of Fortriu' and the 'careful cultivation of the old' has been identified as an innovative feature of the mac-Alpin dynasty. While Forteviot had been the capital of the Picto-Scottish kings, 'Scone of the high shields' seems to have had more ancient associations with Pictish history and ceremonial which prompted its adoption as one of the key centres for the mac-Alpin kings. Similarly, the spiritual centres of the dynasty became focussed on St Andrews and, especially, Dunkeld where Kenneth rebuilt the church founded by an earlier king of Fortriu and endowed it with relics of Saint Columba brought from Iona in 849. While Kenneth's patronage confirmed Dunkeld as the hub of the Columban church in the new kingdom of Alba, it was his 'posthumous patronage' of Iona which most securely established the tradition of the tombs of the kings of Scots in the Reilig Odhrain.

The obituary of Kenneth, son of Alpin, is entered at 858 by both the *Annals of Ulster* and the *Annals of Inisfallen*. The most informative version of the *Chronicle of the Kings* tells how 'he died of a tumour on the ides of February, the third day of the week, in the palace of Forteviot' to which all other manuscripts of the same *Chronicle* add that 'he was buried in the island of Iona, where the three sons of Erc were buried'.

Fergus, Loarn and Oengus, sons of Erc, were the traditional founding dynasts of Scotic Dalriada who crossed from their homeland of Antrim in the last years of the fifth century to establish themselves as kings over the Irish settlement on the western seaboard of Scotland.

The territory claimed by Oengus was centred on the stronghold of Dunyveig on Islay and his brother Loarn held the northern frontier of Dalriada in the lands around the eponymous Firth of Lorne from his power base at Dunollie near Oban. Two of the three clans of Dalriada, the *Cenel Loairn* and *Cenel nOengussa,* were named for the two younger sons of Erc. Ironically the most powerful clan, the royal house based on the capital hillfort at Dunadd on Kintyre, seems never to have been named for its founding dynast Fergus, the eldest son of Erc, whose over-kingship of Dalriada had been prophesied by the 'Apostle of Ireland' himself, according to the *Tripartite Life of Patrick.*

> Patrick said to Fergus: 'Though today thy brother hath little esteem for thee, yet thou shalt be king, and from thee shall come the kings in this country and over Fortriu for ever.'

The obituary of *Fergus Mor,* 'Fergus the Great', is entered at 501 in the *Annals of Tigernach.* However approximate that date, his death must have occurred within just a few years of his coming from Ireland. The brevity of his reign and that of his son Domangart (d. 507) would best explain the dynasty of Dunadd being named the *Cenel Gabrain* for Gabran, grandson of Fergus, whose obituary is reliably entered by the annalist at 559.

Such, then, were the 'three sons of Erc' believed by

the *Chronicle of the Kings* to have been 'buried in Iona'. Therein lies a serious problem of historical reliability and yet one whose solution might resolve some number of enigmas surrounding the tombs of the kings. The earliest sources for the *Chronicle* have been clearly identified as of Irish origin and listing the names and lengths of reign of the kings of Dalriada. These king-lists are of great antiquity and reliability, but they nowhere indicate the place of burial of the kings and neither do the Irish annals include any such note in their royal obituaries. It is only with its entries of Kenneth mac-Alpin and his successors that the *Chronicle of the Kings* adds supplementary historical notes – including his place of burial – to the entry of a king's name and reign-length.

Consequently the monk of St Andrews who first compiled the *Chronicle* in the twelfth century had no known authority for the burial of the sons of Erc on Iona. He may have been working from a lost oral tradition which may itself have preserved evidence surviving nowhere else in the early sources. It may also have been that the burial of kings of Dalriada on Iona was a custom so time-honoured and widely-familiar as to have rendered its inclusion in the Irish annals unnecessary. I, for one, doubt it and especially when only one of the three sons of Erc, the over-king Fergus Mor, was deemed worthy of an obituary by the annalists. Perhaps, now, it might be possible to seek out the source of the tradition of the tombs of the kings.

The four kings known to have been buried on Iona before Kenneth mac-Alpin fall into one of two categories.

The two Irish kings had retired as monks and died the 'straw death' on Iona, so their burial on the island owes nothing to any tradition of ritual royal interment.

The other two kings - Egfrith of Northumbria and Bruide of Fortriu - were both buried during the abbacy of Adamnan, a churchman whose travels and connections in Pictland are well-attested. Both kings, moreover, had ties of kinship to Pictish kings.

Adamnan called Iona 'the Iouan island', a name which has been taken to signify its ancient association with the yew tree held sacred by the pre-Christian druids who were spiritual counsellors to Pictish kings. It is no less significant that Columba, who was granted Iona by a king of Dalriada, made the long and difficult journey to the royal capital of Bruide mac-Maelchon, high-king of Picts, at Craig Phadrig near Inverness to seek his sanction for the foundation of a church on Iona. That itself confirms a Pictish interest in the island, which lay beyond the frontiers of Pictland and within the territory of Dalriada, and such an interest might be explained by its having been held sacred by Pictish tradition of prehistoric antiquity. Iona is formed of the oldest rock in the world such as the druids sought out for their holy places, even for a royal burial-ground long before the coming of Christianity.

It would have been quite characteristic of Adamnan, who is known to have been an accomplished diplomat and intimate of kings, to have fused the Christian and pre-Christian sanctity of Iona by renewing an ancient tradition of Pictish royal burial. It would have been no less characteristic of the mac-Alpin dynasty's 'careful cultivation of the old' to have chosen a burial-ground hallowed by both pagan Pict and Christian Celt for the tombs of its kings, just as Kenneth himself had sited his royal capital in the 'Scone of the high shields' honoured by Pictish tradition.

None of which need have been known to the author of the *Chronicle of the Kings*, writing three hundred years after Kenneth's death. He would have been fully

43

familiar with Iona as the traditional burial-place of kings and might also have viewed that same tradition as one of great antiquity. If the author of the *Chronicle*, or one of his sources which must have post-dated Kenneth's death in 858, had assumed that the royal burials began with the first kings of Dalriada his assumption would not have been wildly unreasonable.

That same assumption might also have lain behind Dean Monro's account of the '48 crowned Scottes Kings' interred in the Reilig Odhrain. The *Chronicle of the Kings* confirms eighteen kings of Scots to have been 'buried in the island of Iona' and it would have been a familiar source book for any thirteenth-century Benedictine abbot of Iona. Had one of them added those eighteen burials to the thirty kings of Dalriada listed in the same *Chronicle* as antecedent to Kenneth mac-Alpin he would have arrived at a total – even allowing for the discrepancies between different manuscripts – approximating to forty-eight 'Scottish' kings. The traditional total of Scottish tombs of the kings, calculated on the basis of quite reasonable historical assumption, would have been passed down the line of his successors until it reached the sixteenth-century prior who so authoritatively informed Dean Monro of the '48 crowned Scottes Kings' entombed 'within this Isle of Kilmkill'.

The same process would similarly account for Dean Monro's total of 'four Ireland Kings' buried in the Reilig Odhrain. Of the 'three sons of Erc' claimed by the *Chronicle of the Kings* to have been buried on Iona only one, Fergus Mor, is acknowledged by the same source as a king of Dalriada. If his two brothers were accounted 'Irish kings' with Niall Frossach and Artgal of Connaught, the total of four occupants of the *Tumulus Regum Hiberniae* would have joined the 'forty-eight' burials in the *Tumulus Regum Scotiae* in the tradition of the tombs of the kings on Iona.

Donald mac-Alpin, king of Scots

Donald, son of Alpin, reigned for four years; and he died at Rath-inver-amon, and was buried in the island of Iona.

Chronicle of the Kings

Donald, son of Alpin (Gael. *Domnall mac-Alpin*), is described by the *Prophecy of Berchan* as 'the wanton son of a foreign wife'.

The first implication of the Berchan 'prophecy' is that Donald was Alpin's son by a woman other than Kenneth's mother, probably a common law or 'handfast' wife or even a concubine. The second is that Donald's mother was of Norse or Norse-Gael stock – on the grounds that Irish sources use the term *gaill* meaning 'foreigner' or 'alien' for the northmen – and would well correspond to the alliance of the mac-Alpin kings with the viking warlords of the Innsegall.

Donald's succession on the death of his brother, or more properly half-brother, Kenneth followed the old style of Irish kingship whereby the claim of the king's brother so often took precedence over that of the king's son. It was a principle of succession which almost inevitably created alternating – and potentially rival – sub-dynasties such as those which were to bedevil the royal house of the sons of Alpin in Alba. Donald himself would seem to have been the first victim of that rivalry on the evidence of a note in the *Verse Chronicle of the Kings**:

He is said to have been assassinated at Scone.

Whatever the nature of Donald's death, its general location is agreed by the sources because *Rath-inver-amon,* 'the fort at the mouth of the river Almond', faces the royal seat at Scone.

For all its brevity, Donald's reign is entered in the *Chronicle of the Kings* as the occasion of the imposition of 'the laws of Aed Find' on Pict as well as Scot. Aed Find (d. 778) is remembered as the great warlord of Dalriada whose invasion of Pictish Fortriu had re-

---

* A variant text included in the 12th-cent. *Chronicle of Melrose.*

46

asserted Dalriadic power after the ferocious Pictish of-
fensive which had conquered Dunadd in 736. His reign
marked the restoration of the kingdom of Dalriada to
the Cenel Gabrain after the temporary ascendancy of
the Cenel Loairn, and the mac-Alpin genealogies were
keen to number him among the eminent royal ancestors
of Alpin and his line.

The precise nature of these 'laws of Aed Find' is
unknown, but they may well have represented the
demand of regular tribute from the subject tribes of
Alba. What is assured is that their 'imposition'
amounted to an important new stage in the establish-
ment of the mac-Alpin dynasty as high-kings of Pict
and Scot alike and thus marked the high peak of the
reign of Donald, son of Alpin.

Constantine I, king of Scots

Constantine, son of Kenneth, reigned for fifteen years; and he was slain by northmen in the battle of Inverdovat, and was buried in the island of Iona.

Chronicle of the Kings

Constantine, Kenneth mac-Alpin's son, succeeded to the kingdom on the death of his father's brother, Donald.

Whether or not Constantine was in any way party to the suspected assassination of his uncle is nowhere recorded, but it must remain a distinct possibility, if only on the evidence from his later reign of his connivance at regicide. By whatever means, Constantine's most remarkable achievement was to hold the kingship of Alba through some sixteen years when the tide of viking conquest of the mainland of Britain reached its flood.

By the second half of the ninth century, the Norse had been firmly established in the northern and western isles of Scotland for at least a generation. Similarly on the Irish mainland, their land-seeking had superseded coastal raiding to the point where Dublin was the effective capital of 'Scandinavian Ireland' within thirty years of its foundation and its Norse overlord recognised in the Irish annals as 'king of the northmen in Erin'. Sea-raiding on the English coast, which had begun so dramatically with the Norse attack on the monastery of Lindisfarne in 793, was followed, and no less dramatically, by the Danish invasion of Northumbria in 866.

By the early 870s, the old Anglo-Saxon kingdom of *Northanhymbre* had given way to a Danish settlement extending as far north as the Tees and centred on York, the *Jorvik* of the northmen. The kingdom of the Scots had become encircled by Scandinavian settlement in the islands to the north and west, across the sea in Ireland, and - most ominously - to the south in Northumbria. Constantine's kingdom, then, was to depend for its survival on alliances with such viking warlords as Olaf of Dublin, described by the sagas as 'the greatest warrior king of the western sea'. Just such an alliance is indicated by the Irish annalist who records Olaf married to a 'daughter of Cináed' [Kenneth

49

mac-Alpin] and thus confirms Constantine's sister as the queen of the Norse king of Dublin.

When Olaf, who had plundered Ireland for fifteen years and to the point of diminishing returns, turned his viking attention to the Scottish mainland he did so as Constantine's ally. In 866, the *Annals of Ulster* record that 'Olaf went into Fortriu, with the gaill of Erin and Alba, when they plundered Pictland and brought away their tributes'. Another Irish annalist tells how 'Pictland was ravaged and plundered by the northmen and they carried off many hostages with them as pledges for tribute'. Whatever Pictish resistance still held out against the overlordship of the mac-Alpin kings could not have withstood the onslaught of Constantine's Norse allies. Much the same fate awaited the proud and ancient stronghold of the Britons of Strathclyde only three years later. In 870, Olaf of Dublin joined forces with Ivar of Jorvik, fresh from his conquest of Northumbria, to besiege Dumbarton Rock and, according to the *Annals of Ulster*, 'at the end of four months destroyed and plundered the fortress'.

All of which must have been watched by Constantine with some satisfaction, if indeed he was not himself militarily involved. The annalist describes Olaf and Ivar returning to the slave-markets of Dublin in 871 'with two hundred ships and a great spoil of people, English, Britons and Picts, brought by them into Ireland in captivity'. It was a slave-haul numbering at least a thousand captives and from which the Gaelic 'men of Alba', Constantine's own people, were conspicuous by their absence.

So also the destruction of Strathclyde served the interests of Constantine's kingdom in finally breaking the power of the north Britons. When Artgal, king of the Britons on Dumbarton Rock, was assassinated in the following year, the annalist notes that he was slain 'at the instigation of Constantine, son of Kenneth', and the way lay open for the Scots' annexation of Strathclyde by the beginning of the tenth century.

He who lived by the sword of the viking was also, in the case of Constantine, to die by it. The alliance of the mac-Alpin dynasty with the Norsemen of Ireland and the Hebrides did not extend to the Danes of Jorvik. Olaf returned to Norway after the siege of Dumbarton, leaving Ivar as king of the northmen at Dublin and Jorvik until his death in 873, when Olaf's son succeeded as king of Dublin and the Jorvik kingdom passed to Ivar's brother, Halfdan the Black.

Halfdan was as ferocious as any of his viking kind and it was his devastation of Northumbria as far to the west as Stainmoor in 875 which drove the community of Cuthbert to abandon their holy island of Lindisfarne. But Halfdan's real ambition lay further afield and his warfleet sailed from the Tyne in the same year on a course which led – by way of the Firth of Forth, overland to the Clyde, and across the North Channel – ultimately to Dublin. Halfdan recognised no alliance with the Scots when his warpath led him through the southern range of Constantine's kingdom and he inflicted a fearsome massacre at Dollar in the Ochils. In the event, Halfdan failed to reclaim his brother's kingship of Dublin in 875 and tried again in 877 only to be slain in a sea-fight on Strangford Lough.

Halfdan's defeated warband made their way back to Northumbria through the Scottish mainland and there unleashed the last of their viking battle-fury. An eleventh-century Irish chronicle* tells of a blood-fray in Fife where 'the earth opened under the men of Alba'. Most prominent among the battle-casualties was their king Constantine, son of Kenneth, who 'fell' – according to the *Prophecy of Berchan* – 'on a Thursday in pools of blood on the shore of Inverdovat'.

* *The War of the Gaedhil with the Gaill*

Aed, king of Scots

Aed, son of Kenneth, reigned for one year; and he was killed by Giric, son of Donald, in the battle of Strathallan, and was buried in the island of Iona.

Chronicle of the Kings

Aed, son of Kenneth mac–Alpin, succeeded his brother as king of Scots in 877. While his reign is entered in the *Chronicle of the Kings* as of one year's duration, there is chronological evidence from variant manuscripts that he survived less than the full twelve months in the kingship.

Nothing is recorded of Aed's reign in Alba other than its brevity and the place and circumstances of his death. The *Chronicle* records that Aed fell in the 'battle of Strathallan', but its most informative text adds that 'he was slain in the township of Nrurim'. The Latinised name–form of *Nrurim* has prompted the identification of the heights of Blairinroar, which divide Strathallan from Glenartney, as the site of the battle. Not only does the *blár–* prefix indicate a battlefield, but upright stones and stone coffins have been found at the farmstead of Blairinroar sited in a pass through the heights.

The battle was a blood–fray between rival branches of the mac–Alpin dynasty. Aed's claim on his elder brother's kingdom was disputed – and perhaps with some justice – by his cousin Giric, eldest son of Donald mac–Alpin, who was able to call on support from his kinsman Eochaid, son of the last Britonic king of Strathclyde.

It was this alliance which defeated Aed's warband above Strathallan and there slew the last son of Kenneth, son of Alpin.

c. AD 889

Giric, king of Scots

Giric, son of Donald, reigned for twelve years; and he died at Dundurn, and was buried in the island of Iona.

Chronicle of the Kings

Giric, son of Donald mac-Alpin, seized the kingdom from his cousin Aed in the battle of Strathallan, but appears to have shared the kingship with his foster-son Eochaid, prince of Strathclyde.

Eochaid, son of Rhun, was the grandson of the Artgal assassinated at the instigation of Constantine in 872. He was also a grandson of the founding dynast Kenneth mac-Alpin, by virtue of his mother who had been a daughter of Kenneth married to Rhun, the last recorded Britonic king at Dumbarton. Eochaid's alliance with his kinsman Giric has been interpreted as the last bid by the Britonic aristocracy of Strathclyde to make good their ancient claim on power in the north. It is not known how power might have been shared between Eochaid and Giric, but it was Giric who stood in the direct lineage of the mac-Alpin dynasty and he, not Eochaid, who was laid in earth on Iona.

Fragments of evidence from English as well as Scottish sources indicate that Giric's territorial ambitions, like those of Kenneth mac-Alpin, lay to the south. The *Chronicle of the Kings* claims that he 'subjugated all Bernicia [the old name for northern Northumbria between Tyne and the Forth] and nearly all the land of the Angles'. The anonymous tenth-century *History of Saint Cuthbert** tells how 'the Scots crossed the Tweed with an innumerable host, wasted Cuthbert's land and despoiled the monastery of Lindisfarne'. Reginald of Durham's history of the *Miracles of Saint Cuthbert* adds that they 'harried every place with slaughter, fire and rapine... spared neither rank, age nor sex, cutting down all like cattle with unheard of cruelty'. Symeon's *History of the Church of Durham* places the same invasion in the time of

---

* Written at Chester-le-Street where the community of Cuthbert took refuge for almost a hundred years before settling in Durham in 995.

55

Guthred, the Christian Dane consecrated king of Jorvik over Saint Cuthbert's coffin in 883, who is credited with defeating the Scots on the unidentified battlefield of *Mundingdene*.

Taken together and allowing for their partisan viewpoints, the evidence of all these sources does confirm a Scots invasion south of the Tweed at some point between 883 and 889. Whether or not Giric sought to take advantage of the instability besetting Anglo-Danish Northumbria following the death of Halfdan, he was certainly extending the range of Kenneth's southern ambitions when he crossed the Tweed. Giric, son of Donald, had effectively launched the conquest of Lothian and the southern uplands which was to dominate the history of north Britain through the following hundred and fifty years.

Much as his father had imposed the laws of Aed Find on Pict and Scot, so it would seem that Giric restored the authority of the Celtic church in his kingdom on the evidence of the *Chronicle of the Kings'* claim that he 'liberated' the Scottish church from Pictish laws and customs. The precise nature of Giric's ecclesiastical reforms is nowhere recorded, but they can be reasonably taken to have enhanced the prestige of Dunkeld as the new royal church of Columba of Iona.

For all his championship of the great saint of the Gael and success as a conquering warlord, Giric was doomed by his association with Eochaid the half-Briton. The *Prophecy of Berchan* bewails 'a Briton placed over the Gael' and the *Chronicle of the Kings* records 'Eochaid and his foster-father expelled from the kingdom' in 889 by an anti-Strathclyde faction led by Donald, son of Constantine.

It is not known how long Giric survived the loss of his kingdom, but he is known to have died at Dundurn, a fort near St Fillans on the Earn, and to have been buried on Iona.

Donald II, king of Scots

Donald, son of Constantine, reigned for eleven years;
and he died in Forres and was buried in the island of
Iona.

Chronicle of the Kings

Donald, son of Constantine, was the first of his dynasty to be styled 'king of Alba' *(rí Albain)* by the Irish annals using a title which had only before been applied – and not since the first years of the sixth century – to the most powerful kings of Scotic Dalriada.

His succession, following the expulsion of Giric and Eochaid in 889, restored the kingship once more to the direct line of Kenneth mac-Alpin and his reign saw the flight of the last members of the Britonic aristocracy from the Clyde to seek refuge in north Wales at the court of the king of Gwynedd.

While Donald annexed Strathclyde as a tributary dominion of Alba under a line of client kings and claimed the Rere Cross on Stainmoor as the southern extent of his kingdom, the Norse, long the masters of Orkney and Shetland, were expanding their control of the northern mainland from Caithness towards the Moray Firth. The ruthless Einar Rognvaldsson – whose traditional discovery of peat-cutting earned him the nickname *Turf-Einar* – was establishing himself as *jarl* of Orkney, and Harald Halfdansson, the king of Norway called 'Finehair', was active in the northern isles.

Conflict between Norse and Scot was inevitable and two blood-frays were of sufficient importance to be entered under Donald's reign in the *Chronicle of the Kings.* One of them is claimed as a Scots victory, but on the second occasion Dunnottar, the coastal stronghold near Stonehaven, 'was destroyed by the northmen'. Such a formidable fortress could only have fallen to a determined onslaught by a substantial warband, perhaps even Harald Finehair's own battlefleet.

Donald himself met his death on the northern frontier of Alba, in Forres according to the *Chronicle,* but not it seems in battle. He died of 'sickness', although the possibility of assassination by poison is mentioned by John of Fordun (c.1380), and was succeeded by his cousin, Constantine, son of Aed.

Constantine II was the first of the mac-Alpin kings to be buried elsewhere than on Iona, but his reign of more than forty years merits its own note here, if only in the interest of continuity.

The changes in the political map of northern England since the time of his grandfather, Kenneth mac-Alpin, focussed Constantine's attention on the southern frontier. Since the time of Alfred the Great (d. 899), the royal house of Wessex had been the great power in an England overshadowed by the Scandinavian settlement centred on Jorvik and where the once-mighty Northumbrian kingdom had dwindled to a tenacious earldom with its power base at Bamburgh.

When the Jorvik Danes were crushed by Wessex at the battle of Tettenhall in 910, the Dublin Norse moved into the resulting power vacuum in the north, invading Northumbria and driving Ealdred, the earl of Bamburgh, into exile at the court of Constantine. If the claims made by the *Chronicle of the Kings* for Giric's conquest south of the Forth still held good twenty years later, Constantine would have been overlord of the Bamburgh earldom and his Scots certainly fought as Earl Ealdred's ally against the Norse at the two battles of Corbridge in 914 and 918. On both occasions the Norsemen won the victory, although their heavy losses in 918 resulted in a truce which passed the kingship of Jorvik to the Norse warlord Ragnall.

The succession of Athelstan as king of Wessex in 924 gave a new impetus to the northern ambitions of the West Saxon kingdom. Athelstan seized control of Jorvik in 927 and, in the same year according to the *Anglo-Saxon Chronicle*, secured the submission of Constantine and lesser kings at Eamont in Cumbria.

This 'submission' amounted to no more than an acknowledgement of territorial boundaries, but Constantine did agree not to support any Norse bid to reclaim Jorvik. Seven years later, he sealed just such an alliance by the marriage of his daughter to Olaf Guthfrithsson, Norse king of Dublin. Athelstan was provoked to a punitive attack on the east coast of Scotland in 934 and Constantine's response was to join Olaf's invasion of northern England which was broken on Athelstan's shield-wall in the blood-fray at Brunanburh in 937.

Olaf did seize Jorvik on the death of Athelstan in 939, but Constantine abdicated in 943 to become a monk at St Andrews and was there laid in earth when he died the 'straw death' in 952.

AD 954

Malcolm I, king of Scots

Malcolm. son of Donald. reigned for eleven years and he was killed by the men of Moray by treachery, and was buried in the island of Iona.

Chronicle of the Kings

Malcolm (Gael. *Máelcoluim,* 'follower of Columba'), son of Donald II, succeeded to the kingship of Alba on the abdication of his cousin, Constantine II, in 943.

Malcolm's reign was dominated, as had been his cousin's, by the rivalry between the West Saxons and the Dublin Norse for control of Jorvik. Olaf Guthfrithsson had died in 941 and been succeeded as king of Jorvik by his cousin Olaf Sitricsson, nicknamed *Olaf Cuaran**, who was driven out by Athelstan's successor, Edmund of Wessex, in 943. Olaf Sitricsson returned to Dublin, but he was back in Scotland after the death of Edmund in 946 and waiting at Scone or Dumbarton to reclaim the kingship of Jorvik.

Just as Constantine had backed Olaf Guthfrithsson in 937, so Malcolm came to the support of Olaf Sitricsson in 949 with an invasion of northern England as far south as the Tees. He seems to have been following not just the example but also the personal encouragement of Constantine, who may even have come out of his monastic retirement for a week 'to visit the English', according to the *Chronicle of the Kings.* In the event, and in the wake of Malcolm's invasion, Olaf did seize the kingship of Jorvik in 949, but the Scots remembered their expedition of that year as 'the raid of the white-backs', most probably a reference to the 'many herds of cattle' brought home as plunder.

Meanwhile and far to the north of the Tay, the 'men of Moray' emerged as the new challenge to the mac-Alpin dynasty and Malcolm led an army into Moray to suppress at least one provincial revolt on his northern frontier. Within a hundred years a *mormaer,* or 'steward', of Moray would win the kingship of Scots**, but even as early as the mid-tenth century the men of Moray brought down a great-grandson of

---

*   see p. 71 below.

**   See **Macbeth**, p. 89 below.

Kenneth mac–Alpin when they slew Malcolm, Donald's son and king of Scots, at Feteresso, near Dunnottar, in the year 954.

AD 962

Indulf, king of Scots

Indulf, son of Constantine [II], reigned for nine years; and he was killed by the Norsemen in Inver-cullen, and was buried in the island of Iona.

Chronicle of the Kings

Indulf, son of Constantine II, succeeded to the kingdom on the death of Malcolm in 954.

His name, from the Norse *Hildulfr,* is as much an example of the extent of Scandinavian influence on the court of his father, Constantine, as was his sister's marriage to a Norse king of York and Dublin. Indulf's earlier succession as sub-king of Strathclyde and Cumbria marks the starting point of a new tradition of 'tanistry' in Scottish kingship. The appointment of a prince of Alba to the sub-kingship in the south-west marked him out as the heir to the kingdom or 'tanist' (Gael. *tanaise,* 'the expected one').

Edmund of Wessex had ravaged Cumbria in 945 in pursuit of Olaf Cuaran, who had taken refuge among the Norse settlement there after being driven from York and before fleeing to Ireland. Tenth-century Cumbria was of much greater extent than the modern county of the same name, extending as far south as the Derwent. Such was the territory ceded by Edmund in 945 to Malcolm, king of Scots. Malcolm, for his part, pledged support 'on land and on sea' to Edmund, who had himself fought beside Athelstan at Brunanburh eight years before. While Malcolm's pledge apparently expired with Edmund (d. 946) on the evidence of his invasion of England in 949, Cumbria remained Scots territory until reclaimed for Norman England in the eleventh century.

The year of Malcolm's death and Indulf's succession marked also the demise of the Jorvik of the northmen. Anglo-Saxon Wessex and Norse Dublin, and with them the Northumbrian earls of Bamburgh, had long jostled for control of Jorvik by means of such rival 'viking kings' as Olaf Cuaran and Erik Bloodaxe, a son of Harald Finehair expelled from Norway. Through fifteen years the kingship of Jorvik passed alternately between Olaf and Erik, each in turn invited, expelled and invited back as the apparent 'lesser of two evils', until Erik was slain in an ambush on Stainmoor in 954.

At which point, the Scandinavian settlement centred on Jorvik was brought under the control of the earls of Bamburgh as client rulers for the Wessex kings. A sub-kingdom extending from the Humber to the Forth was no more viable in the tenth century than it had been two hundred years before, and Indulf took advantage of its most vulnerable northern territory. He seized the formerly Northumbrian fortress of Dun Edin – the future Scottish capital city of Edinburgh – and, by implication, effectively annexed Lothian as far south as the Lammermuir hills and possibly further into the ancient Northumbrian heartland of Bernicia.

The reign of Indulf can be seen as a landmark in the transition of the Dark Age kingdom of Alba into the early medieval Scottish nation, and it is ironic that his death, which brought that reign to its end in 962, was inflicted in a blood-fray straight out of the Dark Ages.

The *Chronicle of the Kings* confirms that Indulf was 'killed by the Norsemen in Inver-cullen and was buried in the island of Iona'. There had been few periods since the end of the eighth century when some part or other of Scotland and its peoples had not suffered the fury of the northmen. Even as late as the mid-tenth century, the remnants of Erik Bloodaxe's warband were raiding the Scottish mainland on their way back to Orkney and the *Chronicle* records 'a fleet of vikings slain in Buchan' in the first years of Indulf's reign. There is saga evidence for settlement of viking warbands – probably out of Orkney or Caithness – in Aberdeenshire by the early 960s. These land-seekers were almost certainly the 'Norsemen' who slew Indulf at 'Inver-cullen', a place which has been most plausibly identified as 'the mouth of the Cullen' in Banff.

On the death of Indulf and in accordance with the tanistry succession, the kingdom of Scots passed to Dubh, son of Malcolm I. and tanist king of Strathclyde-Cumbria since 954.

Dubh, king of Scots

Dubh, son of Malcolm, reigned for four years and six months; and he was killed in Forres, and hidden away under the bridge of Kinloss.

But the sun did not appear so long as he was concealed there; and he was found, and buried in the island of Iona.

Chronicle of the Kings

Dubh, son of Malcolm I, had ruled first as sub-king of Strathclyde and succeeded as high-king of Scots by right of tanistry on the death of Indulf in 962.

His reign of only four years was beset by a new rivalry between the two royal houses whose struggle for the kingdom was to extend into the first decade of the eleventh century. That rivalry grew up between Malcolm's son, Dubh, and Indulf's son, Culen, when Dubh attempted to exclude Culen from succession to the kingship of Scots by excluding him from the tanist kingship of Strathclyde.

Culen's first challenge to Dubh came to battle in Perthshire where both the *mormaer* of Atholl and the abbot of Dunkeld were numbered among the dead. The challenge failed, but Dubh may well have been forced to withdraw northwards into Moray where he faced the second challenge to his kingship and lost. The *Chronicle of the Kings* records Dubh slain at Forres in 966, by Culen's allies if not by Culen himself who succeeded as the next king of Scots..

The strange post-mortal history of Dubh mac-Malcolm – his body hidden under a bridge at Kinloss and darkness over the land until it had been lain in earth on Iona – is more redolent of Gaelic verse than historical record. It does, nonetheless, confirm the great significance of the Reilig Odhrain for the tradition of Scots kingship more than a hundred years after Kenneth mac-Alpin. Bringing Dubh's corpse from Kinloss on the firth of Moray to Iona off the Ross of Mull involved a journey of great hazard over some 180 miles of hostile territory and wild Highland terrain.

If Dubh's short reign contributed little to history, his funeral cortège offers its own testimony to the central theme of these pages. The burial of a king on Iona of Columcille was something far beyond a 'state funeral' formality and the right to a tomb of the kings was not always to be taken up without its own high

69

price of passage. The same right of burial was not to be bestowed on Dubh's successor, Culen, son of Indulf, who is called 'Culenring' by the early sources. While its meaning is uncertain, the suffix has been shown to derive from the Norse *Hringr* and testifies to the Scandinavian influence on the house of Constantine enduring even to the third generation.

Culen reigned for only five years until he was slain – as an act of personal vengeance by Riderch, the son of the sub-king of Strathclyde and son of a nephew of Malcolm I – somewhere in Lothian. His place of burial is unrecorded by the early sources.

AD 981

Olaf 'Cuaran', king of Dublin and York

*Olaf Sitricsson, king of the **gaill** of Dublin, went to Iona in penitence and pilgrimage after the battle of Tara and died there.*

Annals of Tigernach*

* see note p. 26

Olaf, son of Sitric, (ON. *Olafr Sigtryggsson)* is more often called by his nickname of Olaf *Cuaran,* 'Olaf the Sandal', which may well owe something to the footwear characteristic of his monastic retirement on Iona.

He was the son of Sitric *Caech,* 'Sitric the Squint-Eyed', who relinquished the kingship of Dublin to seize the kingdom of Jorvik on the death of Ragnall in 920. Sitric confirmed his kingship by treaty with Athelstan of Wessex in 926, at the same time accepting Christian baptism and sealing the agreement by taking Athelstan's sister as his queen.

Olaf, who was Sitric's son by a previous marriage, claimed his father's former kingdom of Jorvik on the death of his cousin and namesake, Olaf Guthfrithsson in 941. Two years later - and much as his father had done twenty years before - Olaf accepted conversion to Christianity and submission to Wessex. Within the year he was expelled - possibly by pressure from Jorvik northmen resentful of Wessex overlordship, possibly by the king of Wessex who pursued him into Cumbria - and replaced by Erik Bloodaxe, a deposed king of Norway and former jarl of Orkney.

Olaf found his way back to Dublin where he was accepted as king, but he was not able to reclaim Jorvik until 949 when the expulsion of Erik Bloodaxe provided the suitable opportunity and Malcolm of Scotland's invasion of northern England provided the persuasive support for Olaf's return as king of Jorvik.

In the event, his second reign was little better favoured than his first. Within three years, Olaf had been expelled from Jorvik, replaced by Erik Bloodaxe, and reinstated, once again, as king at Dublin. Erik's second reign lasted only two years before he was slain on Stainmoor, but Olaf held the kingdom of Dublin until 980. In that year, the high-king of Ireland succeeded in imposing his authority on the Dublin Norse after his victory in battle at Tara and Olaf

Cuaran fled from his kingdom and into monastic retirement.

Whether or not Olaf was inspired by the example of Constantine II's retirement to St Andrews, his own choice of a monastery willing to provide him with sanctuary cannot have been an easy one. Kells, where the monks of Iona had taken refuge from the viking onslaught for over a hundred and fifty years, would have been unlikely to welcome a royal monk who had plundered its monastic estates as a viking king of Dublin only ten years before.

The submission of the northmen to the 'White Christ' was the inevitable consequence of the pagan land-seekers' contact with the higher civilisation amongst which they settled and, no less inevitably, a lengthy process. Odin, the old god of the viking warband, still held out in the northern isles some two hundred years after the baptism of Aud the Deep-Minded, daughter of a Hebridean viking chieftain and queen of a Norse king of Dublin, in the second half of the ninth century.

Ironically, it was Iona, the holy island so greviously devastated by the initial viking onslaught, which somehow survived to become the spiritual centre of the northmen of Ireland and the Hebrides. By the later tenth century, prominent churchmen, largely independent of Kells, had restored Iona to its ancient prominence as the sacred shrine of the western sea. There it was that Olaf Cuaran came 'in penitence and pilgrimage' in 980 and there he died the 'straw death' of a royal monk - at what must have been a very great age - some twelve months later.

AD 995

Kenneth II, king of Scots

Kenneth, son of Malcolm, reigned for twenty four years; and he was killed. And he is buried in the island of Iona.

Chronicle of the Kings

Kenneth, son of Malcolm I, succeeded to the kingship of Scots following the assassination of Culen, son of Indulf, in 971.

He began his reign – according to the *Chronicle of the Kings* – with the 'plundering of Britain in part' and the 'plundering of England to Stanemore', an invasion of the northern counties intended to confirm Scots dominion over Lothian and Cumbria and declare territorial ambitions for the Northumbrian heartland even as far south as the Tees.

Kenneth's invasion would seem, for all that, to have been less a war of conquest than 'inaugural raiding' of tributary and intended tributary territories, the *crech ríg* which became something of a tradition among early medieval Gaelic kings. Peace had been restored by 973 when Edgar, king of Wessex and effective high-king of England, came to Chester to accept the 'submission' of the lesser kings of the north and west – with Kenneth at their head as high-king in the north – as his 'helpers on sea and land'. Edgar, for his part, would have acknowledged the territorial boundaries of the kingdom of Scots and its southern frontier on the Tweed has been most plausibly dated from the reign of Kenneth II.

Having confirmed the extent of his kingdom, Kenneth's next priority was to secure the succession for his own son, the future Malcolm II. To do so, he needed to exclude the rival mac-Alpin line of Aed from the kingship and, to that end, he slew Olaf, son of Indulf, in 977. The Irish annals describe this Olaf as *Ri Albain*, 'king of Alba', which may well indicate that he ruled for a time in opposition to Kenneth, and most probably in the Isles.

The ruthless elimination of rival claimants to the kingship inevitably spawned factions opposed to Kenneth's ambitions. John of Fordun identifies one of these as the conspiracy hatched by Constantine the

Bald, grandson of Indulf, and Giric, grandson of Dubh, which slew Kenneth II, 'by trickery and craft' according to the *Chronicle,* at Fettercairn in modern Kincardineshire in 995.

Constantine III, king of Scots

Constantine, son of Culen, reigned for one year and six months. And he was killed by Kenneth, Malcolm's son, in Rathinveramon, and was buried in the island of Iona.

Chronicle of the Kings

Constantine 'the Bald', son of Culen and grandson of Indulf, became king of Scots following the death of Kenneth II in 995. The *Prophecy of Berchan* calls him 'the king who will not be king' and his brief reign is significant only as the last appearance in the king-lists by one of the line of Aed, son of Kenneth mac-Alpin.

John of Fordun accuses him of involvement in the conspiracy which brought down Kenneth and his immediate succession as Constantine III does lend support to that allegation, especially when he had every reason to seek vengeance on the rival dynasty which had killed his father and his uncle. Constantine's own reign was to end, in no less violent circumstances and just eighteen months later, when the *Chronicle of the Kings* records him 'killed by Kenneth, Malcolm's son, in Rathinveramon'.

The place of his death can be reasonably identified as the 'fort at the mouth of the river Almond', where it flows into the Tay west of Scone, but 'Kenneth, Malcolm's son' cannot mean Kenneth II, son of Malcolm I, who had been slain in 995. Fordun's identification of Constantine's killer – as an illegitimate son of Malcolm given the same name as his half-brother, Kenneth II – cannot be entirely discounted, but seems less plausible than that proposed by more recent historians. Their explanation is one of a simple scribal error, whereby 'Kenneth, Malcolm's son' is a flawed transcription of 'Kenneth, Malcolm's *grand*son', who succeeded Constantine as Kenneth III and ruled as joint-king with his own son, Giric.

AD 1005

Giric II, king of Scots

Giric, son of Kenneth, son of Dubh, reigned for eight years. He was killed by Kenneth's son [Malcolm II] in Monzievaird; and was buried in Iona.

Chronicle of the Kings

Giric, son of Kenneth, appears to have succeeded to the kingship on the death of Constantine III and to have ruled jointly with his father.

It seems most likely that both father and son fell in the 'battle fought between the men of Scotland on both sides' entered in the *Annals of Ulster* at 1005, but the places of Kenneth's death and burial are unrecorded. Thus the early sources cannot be taken to confirm his burial on Iona. Not so his son Giric, who was slain at Monzievaird – 'the moor of the bards' in Strathearn and quite certainly the site of the battle of 1005 – and is confirmed by the chronicler to have been buried on Iona.

So it was that both Giric II and his father, Kenneth III*, are credited with the same reign-length of eight years by the *Chronicle of the Kings* and the evidence of its variant manuscripts confirms them both slain by the same man.

'His name', according to the *Prophecy of Berchan*, 'is the Aggressor', but history remembers him as Malcolm II.

---

*   'Kenneth, son of Dubh, reigned for eight years' – *Chronicle of the Kings.*

AD 1034

Malcolm II, king of Scots

Malcolm, son of Kenneth, a most victorious king, reigned for thirty years. And he died in Glamis, and was buried in Iona.

Chronicle of the Kings

Malcolm, son of Kenneth II and an Irish princess from the plain of Liffey in Leinster, was the first 'king of Scotland' to have been actually so called. Earlier kings of Scots for a hundred and fifty years had been variously entered in the early sources as kings 'of Fortriu', 'of Picts', and later 'of Alba', but it was Malcolm II whom the contemporary Irish chronicler Marianus Scotus honoured with the title 'king of *Scotia'*.

He was recognised as the most significant king of Scots since the founding dynast Kenneth mac-Alpin by all the earliest sources, not least the *Annals of Tigernach* which call him 'king of Scotland, honour of all the west of Europe'. The *Prophecy of Berchan* describes him as 'voyager of Arran and Islay' which would indicate his overlordship extending into the Hebrides, but it reserves its greatest enthusiasm for Malcolm as warlord, 'heavy-battler of a strong people who will redden weapon-points.'

So indeed he was. Within a year of his succession to the kingship, Malcolm led an invasion as far south as the river Wear to assert the Scots' claim on Northumbria. His target was the new spiritual centre of the northern English at Durham where the community of Cuthbert, driven from Lindisfarne by the northmen some hundred and twenty years before, had finally come to rest in 995.

Sir Walter Scott described Durham Cathedral as 'half house of God, half castle 'gainst the Scot' and such was precisely the intention of the great fortress-shrine above the Wear besieged by Malcolm II in 1006. Symeon of Durham's closely contemporary account of the siege *(De Obsessione Dunelmi* c.1100) tells how Malcolm's blockade was broken by 'the men of Northumbria and Yorkshire' led by Uhtred, son of the aged Earl Waltheof of Northumbria, 'who cut to pieces the entire multitude of the Scots; the king himself, and a few others, escaping with difficulty.'

Malcolm's 'inaugural raid' had failed, and at great cost to his kingdom when Northumbria was able to reclaim some if not all of the lands between the Tweed and the Forth in pursuit of the Scots retreat. Not until twelve years later was Malcolm able to win back the forfeited territories with his momentous victory over the Northumbrian host on the south bank of the Tweed to the east of Carham. Symeon of Durham's account* underlines the historic importance of the battle.

> In the year of our Lord's incarnation ten hundred and eighteen, a comet appeared for thirty nights to the people of Northumbria, a terrible portent of the calamity by which that province was about to be desolated. For, shortly afterwards, nearly the whole population, from the river Tees to the Tweed, and their borders, were cut down in a conflict with a countless multitude of Scots at Carrum.

Malcolm's triumph on the Tweed secured the restoration of Lothian to the kingdom of the Scots, but whatever ambitions he may still have nurtured for the greater conquest of Northumbria were extinguished by Canute, the Danish king of England (1016-1035). Canute's invasion of Scotland in 1031, whether in retribution for Carham or to dispute Malcolm's claim to Cumbria, secured the submission of Malcolm and his mormaers to an Anglo-Danish overlord.

While his submission to Canute would have confirmed Malcolm's border on the Tweed, it seems also to have prompted a decline in his royal prestige. Neither can that prestige have been enhanced by his failure to produce an immediate male heir to his kingdom. Both

*   in Symeon's *History of the Church of Durham.*

of Malcolm's offspring were daughters, one of whom became the wife of the Orkney jarl Sigurd and the mother of the future Jarl Thorfinn the Mighty, while the other, Bethoc, was married to Crinan, the lay abbot of Dunkeld.

Malcolm had reached the great age of at least eighty years by 1034, and while his obituary in the *Chronicle of the Kings* does not indicate his death as by other than natural causes, there are sources which suggest otherwise and which must be taken into account. The evidence of the early sources is at best fragmentary, but there were ancient hatreds in the north ready to feed upon any diminished prestige of the kingship and the 'burning of Dunkeld' entered in the Irish annals at 1027 may be the first sign of internecine feuding which was to bring Malcolm down. The most plausible account which can be distilled from the *Prophecy of Berchan* and the *Chronicle* of Fordun indicates the old king leading an army into the Grampians against a hostile faction from Moray and defeating their warband only to die of his wounds some three days after the blood-fray.

By whatever cause, Malcolm II, the last king of Scots in the direct male line of descent from Kenneth mac-Alpin, died at Glamis on the 25th November in the year 1034 and was buried, as befitted his distinguished lineage, on the island of Iona.

AD 1040

Duncan, king of Scots

Duncan, son of Crinan, abbot of Dunkeld, and of
Bethoc, daughter of Malcolm, Kenneth's son, reigned
for six years. And he was killed by Macbeth, son of
Findlaech, in Bothngouane; and was buried in the island
of Iona.

Chronicle of the Kings

Duncan succeeded to the kingdom on the death of his grandfather, Malcolm II, in 1034. His claim on the kingship through the female line could not go un- challenged, but Malcolm had gone to great lengths to ensure the succession of his daughter's son. He had slain claimants from rival lines of the mac–Alpin dynasty and appointed Duncan as the sub-king of Strathclyde, and thus heir-apparent by claim of tanistry to the kingship of Scots.

Like Malcolm before him – and with no greater success on the evidence of Symeon's *History of the Church of Durham* – Duncan came south in arms and laid siege to Durham in 1039.

> Duncan, king of the Scots, advanced with a count- less multitude of troops and laid siege to Durham, and made strenuous but ineffective efforts to carry it. For a large proportion of his cavalry was slain by the besieged, and he was put to a disorderly flight, in which he lost all his foot-soldiers, whose heads were collected in the market–place and hung up upon posts.
>
> Not long afterwards the same king, upon his return to Scotland, was murdered by his own countrymen.

Whether he was reasserting old territorial ambitions on northern England or dealing out retaliation for the devastation of Cumbria by Eadwulf, earl of North- umbria, in the previous year, some element of kinship- alliance may have lain behind Duncan's disastrous military adventure of 1039.

Eadwulf, son of Earl Uhtred, survived his suc- cessful defence of Durham against Duncan by less than two years. He was slain by Siward the Stout, a Danish warlord based at York and sponsored by King Canute as the rival candidate for the Northumbrian earldom.

Duncan's queen, Suthen, was a close kinswoman – cousin if not sister – to Siward and it would have been fully typical of eleventh-century power politics for Duncan to have attacked Eadwulf's earldom as the ally and agent of his own kinsman-by-marriage.

In the event, Duncan did not live to see Siward claim the Northumbrian earldom from the fallen Eadwulf. Duncan was, indeed and in Symeon's words, 'murdered by his own countrymen' but the full story of his downfall hinges on the enigmatic evidence of the *Orkneyinga Saga.* This history of the Norse jarls of Orkney, set down in Iceland c.1200, tells of the war fought between Jarl Thorfinn and a Scots king given the pejorative Norse name of *Karl Hundason,* 'low-born son of the hound', and identified as the successor to Malcolm II. If Duncan and Karl Hundason were one and the same, then the saga preserves a vivid account of the last year of his reign.

Duncan and Thorfinn can be recognised as rival grandsons of Malcolm locked in a struggle for control of the north of Scotland. When Thorfinn refused to pay tribute for Caithness, Duncan brought his warfleet into the Pentland Firth and suffered defeat in a sea-battle fought off Deerness on the east coast of Orkney. Duncan retreated to the Moray Firth and summoned reinforcements from Ireland – as would have been his right as great-grandson of a Leinster princess – to fight a second battle with the Orkneymen at Tarbat Ness.

Once again, Thorfinn won the victory and at that point Duncan/Karl Hundason disappears from the saga. A Scots king whose claim on the kingship lay through the female line and who had lost three battles within twelve months would have soon fallen prey to hostile factions among his own people. Such would seem to have been the fate of Duncan, who was slain in battle on 15th August 1040 at *Bothngouane,* a place identified as Pitgaveny near Elgin. His sons fled into exile – Malcolm to his mother's kinsfolk in Northumbria and Donald to the Isles – and his kingdom passed to Macbeth, son of Findlaech and mormaer of Moray, as his fruit of victory in the blood-fray.

There can be little doubt that Duncan's fame, even his immortality, rests, as does that of his successor, almost entirely on his fictional representation in Shakespeare's *Macbeth*, but it must be said here that the famous Shakespearean tragedy bears the very least fidelity to the genuine historical record. The historical Duncan was slain by the historical Macbeth, but on the field of battle and not by the assassin's knife whilst asleep in his bed. Neither was Duncan the aged king of the play, but confirmed by the *Annals of Tigernach* as being 'of an immature age' at the time of his death.

There is, nonetheless, at least one point of detail concerning Duncan's fate where Shakespeare is in precise agreement with the historical record of the early sources.

> 'Where is Duncan's body?'
> 'Carried to Colmekill,
> The sacred storehouse of his predecessors
> And guardian of their bones.'

Macbeth, king of Scots

Macbeth, son of Findlaech. reigned for seventeen years. And he was killed in Lumphanan by Malcolm. son of Duncan; and he was buried in the island of Iona.

Chronicle of the Kings

Macbeth is, without a doubt, the best-known of all the kings buried on Iona, for no other reason than his inclusion as the central character of the eponymous Shakespeare play and despite the fact of there being no resemblance between the fictional Macbeth and his historical counterpart.

The historical Macbeth (Gael. *Macbethad*, 'son of life'), son of Findlaech, first appears in the early sources as the 'king', called *Maelbaethe* by the *Anglo-Saxon Chronicle*, who submitted with Malcolm II to Canute in 1031. The hereditary office of *mormaer* or 'great steward', effectively that of a provincial sub-king akin to a Norse *jarl*, is first mentioned by the early sources to identify an allied warlord of Constantine II at the battle of Corbridge in 918, and there are further references to mormaers through the later tenth century. Macbeth's father, Findlaech, had been mormaer of Moray until 1020 when he was slain by his nephews - Malcolm, who followed him as mormaer, and Gillecomgain who became mormaer on the death of Malcolm in 1029. Gillecomgain held on to power for little more than two years until Macbeth, son of Findlaech, was able to enforce his hereditary claim at some point prior to 1031. Thus he had ruled for some ten years in Moray before he slew Duncan, son of Crinan, to seize the kingship of Scots in 1040.

While his burial among the tombs of the kings on Iona serves as confirmation of the legitimacy of Macbeth's right to that high-kingship, the precise nature of his claim is far from clear. His queen, Gruoch - the historical 'Lady Macbeth' - had been earlier married to Gillecomgain and her second marriage to Macbeth would have confirmed the ending of the power struggle within Moray. Gruoch was also a granddaughter of Kenneth III, the king of Scots who had been slain by Malcolm II in 1005, and would have thus provided Macbeth with a claim by marriage on the kingship of Scots. His marriage to Gruoch would have drawn Macbeth into the feud between rival branches of the mac-Alpin dynasty, but his killing of Duncan and seizure of the kingship might be shown to have its deepest roots in the earlier history of Scotic Dalriada*.

There had been dynastic rivalry between the Dalriadic royal house of the Cenel Gabrain and the lesser lineage of the Cenel Loairn even as early as the end of the sixth century. By the last quarter of the seventh century, the Cenel Loairn had seized the kingship of Dalriada from the Cenel Gabrain and held it until c.736 when it was reclaimed by Aed Find for the line of Gabran. When the viking onslaught, which first engulfed the western seaboard in the last decade of the eighth century, drove the Dalriadic kings east into Tayside, the rival Cenel Loairn was driven north up the Great Glen. While the Cenel Gabrain had imposed themselves as rulers of the Pictish kingdom of Fortriu, so the Cenel Loairn established themselves in the more ancient Pictish power base north of the Mounth, from which they were to re-enter history in the tenth century as the mormaers of Moray, a territory extending north into Ross and bounded by the river Spey in the east and in the west by Loch Alsh.

So it was that the hostility between the later generations of the royal house of mac-Alpin and the sub-kings of Moray had its roots not only in the ancient feud between the Cenel Gabrain and Cenel Loairn, but may also have reflected the still older rivalry between northern and southern kingdoms of Pictland. Thus, Macbeth mac-Findlaech, mormaer of Moray, could have claimed the high-kingship of Scots as the victorious heir to the power struggles of centuries past.

---

* see the **Sons of Erc**, p. 41 above.

The ancient Celtic tradition reflected in the *Prophecy of Berchan* is quite unequivocal in its celebration of his succession.

The Red King will take the kingdom ... the ruddy-faced, yellow-haired, tall one, I shall be joyful in him. Scotland will be brimful, in the west and in the east, during the reign of the furious Red One.

The historical record of Macbeth's reign fully supports Berchan's portrait of a tall warrior king, generous and indomitable. Early Scottish sources confirm the generosity of his land-grants to the Culdees of Loch Leven and even the *Anglo-Saxon Chronicle* tells of Macbeth 'scattering money like seed' on his pilgrimage to Rome in 1050.

Such journeys overseas would not have been undertaken by a king who was less than confident in the security of his kingdom, and Macbeth's pilgrimage attests his popularity as much as his power. His power was nonetheless underwritten by his alliance with the Orkney Norse, and specifically with Jarl Thorfinn II, remembered as Thorfinn the Mighty. Macbeth's own heartland of Moray lay on the southern frontier of the Norse settlement of the Scottish mainland where he must have achieved some form of co-existence with the thrusting ambition of the Orkney jarldom. It had been Thorfinn's war on Duncan which opened the way for Macbeth's seizure of the kingdom and, having despatched their common enemy, they divided up his former kingdom between them.

All of which concentrated Macbeth's enemies in the south, where Duncan's son Malcolm had fled in 1040 to find refuge with his mother's kinsman, Earl Siward of Northumbria. Five years later, Siward invaded Scotland in support of Abbot Crinan's bid to overthrow Macbeth. In the event, both the invasion and the uprising were defeated by Macbeth and his Norse allies near Dunkeld, in a blood-fray described by the *Annals of Tigernach* as a 'battle between the men of Alba on both sides, in which Crinan, abbot of Dunkeld, was slain and many with him'. Macbeth was thus secured in his kingdom for the greater part of a decade, during which time Duncan's son Malcolm was growing to manhood in his Northumbrian exile.

By 1054, Malcolm was ready to present himself as a rival for the kingship of Scots, and his kinsman, Earl Siward, was no less ready to back up his claim with an Anglo-Danish invasion force. This second challenge to Macbeth's kingdom met with much greater success than the first. Siward's fleet entered the Tay and his army crossed the Forth at Stirling to join forces in Strathearn and strike for the royal capital. The *Prophecy of Berchan* tells of an 'eruption of blood in the midst of Scone' and the *Anglo-Saxon Chronicle* of how 'Earl Siward fought against the Scots of whom he made great slaughter and put them to flight, but their king escaped. Many also fell on his own side, both Dane and English ... on the day of the Seven Sleepers, that is on the 27th July'. The victory, although won at such great cost, reclaimed Lothian, and with it Fife and Strathclyde-Cumbria, for Duncan's son and forced Macbeth to retreat to his heartland of Moray. Siward was to survive the great battle by no more than a year, but Macbeth held out in his northern fastness for three more years until Malcolm was sufficiently powerful to bring him to bay at Lumphanan in Mar.

There Macbeth was slain in battle by Duncan's son on the 15th August 1057, seventeen years to the day since he himself had slain Duncan to seize the kingship of Scots.

Lulach, king of Scots

Lulach the Fool reigned for four months.
And he was killed in Essie in Strathbogie;
and was buried in the island of Iona.

Chronicle of the Kings

Lulach, son of Gillecomgain. was proclaimed king of Scots by the men of Moray following the death of Macbeth at the hands of Malcolm. son of Duncan. on the 15th August 1057.

It is not known precisely why the *Chronicle of the Kings* calls him *Lulach Fatuus*. 'Lulach the Fool', but it would seem to have been a derisory nickname posthumously endowed on a king whose brief reign marked the last resistance of the old Celtic tradition of kingship.

Lulach was descended from the royal house of mac-Alpin through his mother, Gruoch, and from the ancient line of tribal kings of Moray through his father, Gillecomgain. Lulach himself had ruled Moray as mormaer during the reign of his step-father Macbeth as king of Scots, and his burial on Iona is firm evidence that he was regarded as a legitimate successor to an ancient line of Scottish kings.

In terms of the *realpolitik* of eleventh-century Scotland, Lulach's destruction would have been the most urgent priority for Malcolm after the fall of Macbeth. In the event, it took four months to hunt Lulach down in his ancestral heartland of Moray where he was slain by Malcolm at Essie in Strathbogie, Aberdeenshire. in the first days of 1058.

Thus Malcolm, son of Duncan, reclaimed his father's kingdom as Malcolm III, king of Scots. He is most often called Malcolm 'Canmore' from his Gaelic cognomen *Ceann Mor*, which is sometimes translated as 'The Great Chieftain', but – because Gaelic nicknames almost always refer to physical characteristics – more probably describes 'Malcolm of the Great Head'.

His thirty-two year reign can be said to mark the beginning of medieval Scotland and this was in no small part due to the influence of Malcolm's second queen. Margaret. She was the mother of three future Scottish kings and, still more importantly, it was she who opened up the Scottish church, state and society to a shape-changing influx of English and continental European cultures.

Ironically, it was this future Saint Margaret of Scotland who built the Saint Odhran's Chapel on Iona, and her husband King Malcolm who brought the long tradition of the Reilig Odhrain as the burial-ground of Scotland's kings to its end.

Malcolm ruled Scotland while the Normans conquered England and he invaded Northumbria on no fewer than five occasions. He was returning from his fifth invasion when he was ambushed by the Norman overlord of Northumbria, Robert de Mowbray, and slain by de Mowbray's nephew, Arkil Morel, near Alnwick on the 13th November 1093.

He was buried first at the priory of Tynemouth and only later were his remains brought back to Scotland by his son and eventual successor, Alexander I (king of Scots 1107-1124). There they were re-interred but not among the tombs of the kings on Iona. Malcolm's final resting-place was beside that of Queen Margaret in the church of the Holy Trinity they had founded together at Dunfermline.

Duncan II, king of Scots

&

after AD 1097

Donald III, king of Scots

Donald, son of Duncan, first reigned for six months, and was afterwards expelled; and Duncan, son of Malcolm, reigned for six months. Duncan was killed at Mondynes, by Malpetair, earl of Mearns, and lies in the island of Iona*, and Donald, son of Duncan, reigned again for three years.

Donald was captured by Edgar, son of Malcolm, was blinded and died at Rescobie. He was buried at Dunkeld; and his bones were removed thence to Iona.

Chronicle of the Kings

---

* Duncan's burial on Iona is entered in only one manuscript of the *Chronicle*.

Donald and Malcolm, the sons of Duncan, had fled into exile when their father was slain by Macbeth in 1040. While Malcolm took refuge in Northumbria, Donald found sanctuary in the Hebrides. There he came under the influence of the Gaelic-Norse culture of the isles, an influence clearly reflected in his Gaelic name of *Domnall Bàn*, 'Donald the Fair', and the fact that he is the only king to be identified by his real name in the Gaelic-derived *Prophecy of Berchan*.

In consequence, Donald's seizure of the kingship on the death of his brother in 1093 prompted a resurgence of the Gael against the Anglo-Norman culture espoused by Malcolm Canmore and his English queen Margaret, who had died of grief just four days after her husband was slain in Northumbria. Their sons fled into exile in England and the *Anglo-Saxon Chronicle* confirms that Donald 'drove out all the English who were with King Malcolm before'.

None of which endeared Scotland's new Gaelic restoration to William Rufus, son of the Conqueror, who had succeeded his father only four years earlier. Malcolm Canmore's relations with Norman England had been less than friendly, not least on account of his territorial ambitions towards Northumbria, but he had more than once acknowledged Norman overlordship and had even given up his eldest son, Duncan, as guarantee of his own good behaviour.

Duncan was Malcolm's son by his first queen Ingibjorg (d. 1068), the widow of Jarl Thorfinn of Orkney. He had been sent south in 1072 as a hostage following Malcolm's submission to William I at Abernethy. Duncan had been held prisoner until the death of William I in 1089, when he was released by William Rufus on his succession as William II, and knighted by another son of the Conqueror, Robert 'Curthose', duke of Normandy.

So it was that when William II looked for a Scots challenge to Donald III he needed to look no further than Duncan mac-Malcolm. At some point between the last months of 1093 and the spring of 1094, an Anglo-Norman invasion force marched north into Scotland to depose Donald and install his nephew Duncan as the new king of Scots. Duncan II survived in the kingship for only six months according to the *Chronicle of the Kings*. His brief reign was doomed by a violent anti-Norman reaction and he was dead by the end of the year, slain on Donald's instigation by the mormaer of Mearns at Mondynes near Stonehaven.

It is unusually suspicious that only one manuscript of the *Chronicle* identifies his place of burial as Iona. If that identification is accurate and Duncan II was interred in the Reilig Odhrain, then it is an extraordinary paradox to find a king of Scots who lived the greater part of his life in Norman England, who was trained as a Norman knight and knighted by a Norman duke, laid in the earth of the most sacred shrine of the Gael.

No such paradox attends the burial of his uncle, Donald Bàn, whose final resting place is well confirmed by the early sources.

Donald was already sixty years old and an aged man by early medieval standards when he first succeeded Malcolm in 1093. His advanced years made his hold on the kingdom ever more precarious when he was restored to the kingship on the death of his nephew. He nonetheless held on to power for three more years until a second challenge brought his reign, and with it his life, to an end.

Duncan's half-brother Edgar, the eldest of Queen Margaret's sons, had found sanctuary at the court of William Rufus in 1093 and was more than willing to become William's vassal king in Scotland. The English sources consider him to have been the rightful king of Scots by 1095 and two years later he led a Norman army north across the Tweed to seize the kingdom from his uncle. His first acts as king were to make Donald captive, to put out his eyes and afterwards put him to death at Rescobie near Forfar in 1097.

Donald Bàn was buried first at Dunkeld, but later reburied on Iona. The precise date of his last interment is unknown, but it was certainly earlier and probably some decades earlier than 1150. He was the last king of Scots to be laid in earth, even as an afterthought, in the Reilig Odhrain of I-Columcille.

Godred Olafsson, king of Man and the Isles

In the same year [1187]. on the tenth of November.
Godred, King of the Isles, died in the Island of Saint
Patrick, in Man.   In the beginning of the following
summer his body was removed to the Island called
Iona.

Chronicle of Man*

---

* The Chronicle of Man and the Sudreys (from Sudreyjar, or
'Southern Isles', the Norse name for the Hebrides) was compiled in
the monastery of St Mary at Rushen on the Isle of Man and
completed in the 14th century.

Godred, son of Olaf the Red, is the one Norse king of Man whose burial on Iona is confirmed by the sources and can, thus, be numbered as one of the 'eight Norse kings' traditionally interred in the *Tumulus Regum Norwegiae.*

The Isle of Man had been a viking lair since the first wave of Scandinavian sea-raiding had broken through the North Channel in 795, but only after the power of the Dublin Norse had been finally broken by the Irish high-king Brian Boru at the battle of Clontarf in 1014 did the 'Kingdom of Man and the Sudreys' emerge as the northmen's new power base in the western sea. This Norse kingdom of Man reached the peak of its ascendancy under the dynasty founded in the second half of the eleventh century by Godred *Crovan* - 'Godred the Pale' from the Irish *cró-bain,* literally 'the white blooded'.

He was the son of the Norse chieftain Harald the Black of Islay and had fought with Harald Hardradi's force at Stamford Bridge in 1066. While the Hebridean contingent suffered heavily in Hardradi's defeat, Godred somehow escaped the carnage to find refuge on Man and set his ambition on seizing the kingdom for himself. His chance came with the death of its reigning king in 1070, when he usurped the succession to found the dynasty which was to rule Man and the Isles for the greater part of a hundred years. Godred Crovan's death in 1086 led to a feud between his sons out of which the eldest, Lagman, emerged as victor after killing his brother Harald. The third son, Olaf, was still a minor when Lagman died on a penitential pilgrimage to Jerusalem in 1095, so the chieftains of the isles turned to the Irish high-king to appoint a regent. The regency lasted only three years until the tyranny of the Irish appointee prompted the island chieftains to drive him out.

All this turbulence in the western sea aroused the

predatory interest of Magnus Bareleg, king of Norway, who brought his warfleet into the Hebrides in 1098 to ravage the islands and claim the seaboard from Lewis down to Islay and Kintyre as Norwegian territory. Magnus' ambition led him to demand the overlordship of Ireland, but he had over-reached himself and he was cut down with his warband by an Irish host in Ulster in 1103. The chieftains turned once again to the Crovan dynasty – in the person of Godred's third son, Olaf the Red, who had reached maturity by 1104 and ruled as king of Man and the Sudreys for some fifty years until he was assassinated by his nephews in 1153.

Olaf's eldest son Godred was in Norway when he learned of his father's downfall. He immediately returned to Man, where he executed the assassins and established himself as king. He was to prove himself the most piratical and oppressive of his dynasty, raiding Ireland in the old viking way and antagonising the Hebridean chieftains to the point where they looked to one of their own kind to take a stand against the king of Man.

The islands of the western sea had suffered grievously from the successive onslaughts of latter-day viking warlords who were drawn into the power vacuum left by the collapse of the Dublin Norse after Clontarf. Jarls of Orkney, kings of Man, and – perhaps most ferocious of all – King Magnus Bareleg of Norway had, each in turn, ravaged the isles in pursuit of their territorial ambitions. Not until the twelfth century – when civil wars in Scandinavia distracted Norwegian kings from Hebridean adventuring for some hundred years – was it possible for the Islesmen to assert their real independence and present the Norse of Man with a serious rival in the person of Somerled*, 'king of the Isles' and founding dynast of the Clan Donald.

* see also p. 110 below.

It was to Somerled that the Hebridean chieftains turned for their challenge to the oppressions of Godred of Man and proclaimed Somerled's son, Dugald, over-lord of the Isles. Godred immediately prepared for battle with Somerled's fleet of eighty warships and the rival forces came together in the waters to the west of Islay where they fought through the night of Epiphany [5/6th January] 1156. When dawn broke to reveal terrible carnage but no clear victor, they were forced to a negotiated settlement whereby the kingdom of Man and the Sudreys was divided between them. The warlords of early Scotland were rarely satisfied with diplomatic compromise and in 1158 Somerled tried again, bringing a fleet of fifty-eight ships through the North Channel to inflict a decisive defeat on the Manx Norse. Godred took flight to find refuge in Norway, while the Islesmen wreaked their vengeance by laying waste the Isle of Man.

Thus Somerled won the overlordship of the isles from the kings of Man, but his greater ambition lay in restoring to himself the full extent of the old kingdom of Scotic Dalriada. It was an ambition which inevitably brought him into conflict with Malcolm IV (king of Scotland 1141-1165) and, no less inevitably, brought him down. When Somerled was killed at Renfrew in 1164, Godred's brother lost no time in seizing back the isles for the kingdom of Man, but his brief reign came to a sudden end in the same year when Godred re-turned from Norway to cruelly punish the usurper and restore himself as king of Man and the Isles.

Godred reigned again – and relatively peacefully apart from an attempted coup which was swiftly and violently suppressed in 1182 – for a further twenty-three years until his death on 'Saint Patrick's' [Peel] Island off the shore of Man on the 10th November 1187. In the following summer, according to the *Chronicle of Man,* 'his body was removed to the Island

104

called Iona'.

Precisely why Godred Olafsson's remains should have been reburied in the Reilig Odhrain is unknown, because there was certainly no evident tradition of burial on Iona associated with the kings of Man. His grandfather, the dynast Godred Crovan, had been buried on Islay and both his father, Olaf, and his son, Ragnvald, were entombed at Rushen, so the choice of Iona for Godred's final resting-place is most probably to be interpreted as a political gesture.

While the burial of Malcolm Canmore at Dunfermline had effectively put an end to the ancient tradition of the burial of kings of Scots in the Reilig Odhrain, the patronage of Somerled and his sons had newly established Iona as the dynastic church of the lordship of the Isles. In the light of that, the choice of the holy island of the western sea for the tomb of Godred of Man can only have been intended as a posthumous gesture of triumph on behalf of Somerled's great rival.

AD 1230

Uspak 'Hakon', Norse king of the Isles.

Hakon, king of Norway, had appointed a certain nobleman of royal lineage, by name Uspak, son of Owmund, as king over the Sodor Islands [Hebrides] and gave him the name of 'Hakon'.

    This 'Hakon' went with ... a great force of Norsemen, to the Sodor Islands. When they came to the island called Bute and sought to storm the castle which is in it, 'Hakon' was struck by a stone and killed, and he was buried in the island of Iona.

Chronicle of Man

Uspak - called 'Hakon' by the Norse - was, in fact, the son of a son of Somerled*. He had left the Hebrides in his youth to seek his fortune in Norway and appears to have returned to the Isles as a sea-raider on at least one occasion some twenty years before he came west-over-sea to reclaim the Isles for the Norse.

The deaths of Somerled in 1164 and of Godred, king of Man, in 1187 had left a number of rival sons and heirs whose feuding dominated the following half-century of Hebridean history. Ragnvald Godredsson (d. 1229) had followed his father as king of Man, but his reign had been disrupted by conflict with his brother Olaf, lord of Lewis and the Outer Hebrides. Their intermittent feuding was aggravated first by Ranald, Somerled's eldest son and successor, who took the part of Ragnvald and delivered Olaf to be imprisoned by the Scots king William the Lion, and later by Donald, son of Ranald, whose piracy extended to raiding the Irish mainland.

All of which resulted in 'a great dispeace' in the Hebrides and prompted Hakon Hakonsson, king of Norway, to appoint his own overlord for the Isles in the person of Uspak, grandson of Somerled. In the year 1230, Uspak - whose *nom-de-guerre* of 'Hakon' reflects his client relationship to the king of Norway - brought a fleet of eighty longships into the Sound of Islay where he joined forces with 'a great company' led by his brothers, Dugall and Duncan of Lorne.

The accounts of the expedition preserved in the *Chronicle of Man* and *Hakon Hakonsson's Saga* are less than lucid, but it appears that Uspak had to rescue his brothers from violence which erupted between Norsemen and Islesmen in the course of 'feasting' before he could press on with the expedition. His target, it seems, was the Isle of Bute and its castle

---

* Dugald mac-Somerled, called *Owmund* or *Ogmund* by the Norse.

was duly laid siege until a rock cast down by its defenders brought to its end the brief reign of 'Uspak surnamed Hakon' as Norse king of the Isles.

Uspak died of his injuries and was buried among the tombs of the kings on Iona, the same 'holy island' which he had visited - according to the sagas* - as a sea-raider in 1209.

> That summer ... Uspak the Hebridean went a-viking west-over-sea. And they plundered in the Sudreyjar while the kings in the isles fought a civil war amongst themselves.
>
> They pillaged the holy island ... and those that came back to Norway were sternly rebuked by the bishops for their piracy.

Ironically, and however doubtful his claim to the title, Uspak 'Hakon' was the last 'king' whose burial on Iona is confirmed by the early sources.

---

* *Hakon Sverrisson, Guthorm and Ingi's Saga* included with *Hakon Hakonsson's Saga* in the 13th century *Eirspenill* manuscript.

'OTHER PERSONS OF DISTINCTION
ALL DONE IN ARMOUR'

The Tombs of the Chieftains

The tradition of Iona as the burial-place of kings was so deeply rooted in the Celtic foundations of Scottish kingship that it would, almost inevitably, be abandoned with the shift away from the Celtic wellsprings which characterised the reign of Malcolm Canmore.

The choice of Dunfermline for Malcolm's own final resting place marks the end of a tradition of royal burial which had been a part of Scottish kingship for more than two hundred years and all of his sons who succeeded as the new 'mac-Malcolm' dynasty of kings of Scots - with the single and uncertain exception of Duncan II - are known to have been buried elsewhere than the Reilig Odhrain. The fact that the only successor to Malcolm who can be confirmed to have been laid in earth on Iona was his brother, Donald Bàn, has its own prophetic significance, because Donald was a creature of the same Gaelic-Norse culture of the Isles which was to cherish the tradition of the Reilig Odhrain for centuries after the last king of Scots had been buried on Iona.

While the kingdom of Scots moved into the Anglo-Norman orbit of the twelfth century, the Isles held out as the last fastness of Celtic Scotland and while the mac-Malcolm kings looked south of the Forth and attracted Norman knights to form the core of the new Scots aristocracy, a new resurgence of the Gael was reclaiming the western seaboard from the northmen. At its centre stood the extraordinary figure of the warlord Somerled, son of Gillebride.

The origins of the historical Somerled are no less enigmatic than those of Macbeth or Kenneth mac-Alpin, but all the evidence marks him out as typical of the Gaelic-Norse aristocracy which had emerged in the west by the twelfth century. His father had been an influential supporter of Donald Bàn's claim on the kingship, but his Norse name meaning 'summer voyager' bears clear testimony to his viking forbears and his wife, Ragnhilda, was a daughter of Olaf the Red, Norse king of Man. The genealogies proclaim Somerled to have been seventh in direct descent from Guthfrith mac-Fergus, the ninth-century viking chieftain of the Hebrides and ally of Kenneth mac-Alpin, and yet the proudest claim of his dynasty was its descent from the semi-legendary Irish chieftain, Conn of the Hundred Battles.

It is a remarkable coincidence that it was at much the same time of the mid-twelfth century when the scribes at St Andrews were constructing the descent of the mac-Alpin kings from the Cenel Gabrain of Dalriada that the *seannachies** in the Isles were tracing the lineage of the house of Somerled back to the Clan Colla who colonised the western seaboard from Ireland – according to Irish legend – long before the arrival of the Sons of Erc.

What is beyond dispute is that Somerled mac-Gillebride was the forbear of the mighty Clan Donald and founder of the dynasty which was destined to inherit the tradition of the tombs of the kings.

Which is not to say that all the Lords of the Isles and

---

* literally 'story-tellers' but effectively Clan historians and genealogists

chieftains of the clans were buried on Iona and neither is it possible to identify accurately a full list of those who were, because so much of the evidence is preserved in tradition rather than any more formal historical record.

There are just two principal written sources for later medieval interments in the burial-ground of the kings. One is the *Book of Clanranald* which was compiled by generations of MacVurichs, hereditary seannachies to Clan Donald, and the second is the *History of the Macdonalds* set down in the seventeenth century by another seannachie, Hugh Macdonald of Sleat.

A complementary – and quite indisputable – source is the evidence of the gravestones of the Reilig Odhrain, some number of which are still to be seen on Iona and were even more clearly legible at the end of the seventeenth century when Martin Martin entered them in his *Description of the Western Islands of Scotland*. It was, of course, Martin who supplied this chapter with its title when he described the stones carved with armoured figures as marking the tombs of 'other Persons of Distinction ... all done in Armour'.

None of these sources can confirm that Somerled lies buried in the hallowed earth of Iona. He is known to have generously endowed the church there, and the Saint Odhran chapel especially, but tradition claims his tomb for the priory at Saddell on Kintyre. Nonetheless, Hugh Macdonald's account of the killing of Somerled by the henchmen of Malcolm IV (king of Scotland 1153-65) adds a note of the king's final homage to the fallen warlord.

The king sent a boat with the corpse of Somerled to Icolumkill at his own charges.

The most plausible explanation might be that Somerled was first buried on Iona in 1164 and soon afterwards re-buried at Saddell - where a carved stone has long been believed to mark his tomb - when the priory was founded there by his son Ranald.

Ranald mac-Somerled, who succeeded to much of his father's overlordship of the Isles and Kintyre, was the first of the dynasty confirmed by the *Book of Clanranald* to have been buried on Iona.

> Ranald was the most distinguished of the gaill or the Gael for prosperity, sway of generosity, and feats of arms.
> Three monasteries were erected by him, that is a monastery of Black Monks in Iona, in honour of God and Columcille; a monastery of Black Nuns in the same place; and a monastery of Grey Friars at Saddell, and it is he also who founded the monastic order of Molaise.
> ... He died and was buried at Reilig Odhrain in Iona in the year of our Lord 1207.

So also - on the evidence of Martin Martin's reading of an inscribed stone he found in the ruined Nunnery on Iona - was Ranald's sister, the prioress **Bethoc.**

> Another Inscription is; *Behag Nijn Sorle vic Il vrid Priorissa:* that is Bethoc, Daughter to Somerled, son of Gillebride, Prioress.

Ranald's son and successor was the piratical **Donald of Islay** (Gael. *Domhnall*) for whom Clan Donald was named.   He died in 1249 and while the *Book of Clanranald* does not record the place of his death or burial, the Sleat historian is confident of both locations.

He died at Shippinage [Skipness, Kintyre] ...
and was buried at Icolumkill.

Much the same is true of his son and successor,
Angus Mor, the 'Great Angus' who died in 1292. The
Book of Clanranald records that he died on Islay with
no note of his place of burial, but Macdonald of Sleat
clearly had access to more precise sources of
tradition.

He died at Kilcummin [Kilchoman] in Islay ... and,
with the accustomed solemnity of his predecessors,
was buried at Icolumkill.

Angus Mor was followed as overlord of the Isles by his
son and namesake Angus Og ('Young Angus') whose
burial on Iona is most impressively documented.

Angus Og (d. c.1327) ruled the Isles through the
tumultuous years of William Wallace, Robert Bruce and
the Scottish Wars of Independence. It was Angus who
led the Islesmen to fight for the Bruce at Bannockburn
in 1314. On the eve of the battle, King Robert is said
to have told Angus that 'my hope is constant in thee',
and after the victory expressed his gratitude with
generous land-grants to the lordship.

'This Angus of the Isles' was described by the *Book
of Clanranald* as 'the noble and renowned chief of the
Innsigall ...'

This Angus Og died in Islay, and his body was
interred in Iona.

He was, it seems, actually buried in the *Teampull
Odhrain*, 'Saint Odhran's Chapel', and it was there that
Martin Martin found his tombstone carved with the
galley of Clan Donald and the confirming inscription:

113

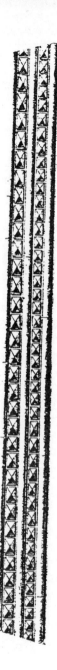

114

Hic Iacet Corpus Angusii Filii
Domini Angusii macDomnill de Ila

Here lies the body of Angus,
son of the lord Angus, son of Donald of Islay

The lordship of the Isles had been an effective dominion
since the time of Somerled, but it was not until the
succession of the son of Angus Og that one of the
house of Somerled was actually endowed with the formal title of Lord of the Isles.

Somerled had been styled *rex insularum*, 'king of
the isles', and he and his successors had no less
reasonable claim on royal title than had the Kings of
Man. In real terms, however, their political power was
that of a mormaer, or at best a 'sub-king', who paid
allegiance as occasion demanded to the kings of Norway
and the kings of Scots. Their independence hinged on
playing off one over-king against another until the
Norse relinquished their claim on the Hebrides after the
battle of Largs in 1263. Thereafter the overlords of
the Isles played their own part in the struggle between
the rival factions claiming the Scottish kingship, placing
their loyalty and alliance wherever they felt they had
most to gain. Thus the house of Somerled remained a
power in the land for more than three hundred years,
but it was only in the second quarter of the fourteenth
century that their vast dominion from the Isle of Lewis
down to the Mull of Kintyre was recognised by the
Treaty of Alliance of 1335

So it was that **John of Islay** became the first Lord
of the Isles. He died in 1380 and his burial on Iona is
confirmed by the *Book of Clanranald* in a passage rich
in descriptive detail.

He died in his own castle of Ardtornish, while
monks and priests were over his body, he having

received the body of Christ and having been anointed, his fair body was brought to Iona of Columcille, and the abbot and the monks and vicars came to meet him, as it was the custom to meet the body of the king of Fionngall*, and his service and waking were honourably performed during eight days and eight nights, and he was laid in the same grave with his father in Teampull Odhrain in the year of our Lord 1380.

The second Lord of the Isles was **Donald,** son of John of Islay, who is remembered as 'Donald of Harlaw' in recognition of the battle of 1411 where he led the Islesmen in support of his vow to 'lose all he had or to gain the Earldom of Ross'.

The death of Robert III (king of Scotland 1390–1406) had been followed by the regency of his brother, the Duke of Albany, and Donald seized the opportunity to press his wife's claim on the disputed earldom. When the Regent Albany refused, Donald called a great hosting in the Isles to take Ross by force. The dispute came to battle on 24th July at Harlaw a few miles north of Inverurie where Donald's 10,000 Islesmen and Highlanders fought through the afternoon and into the evening against the Regent's army under the Earl of Mar. The battle was effectively a stalemate, despite both sides claiming the victory, and it is remembered principally for the great slaughter which entered it into tradition as 'Red Harlaw'.

---

* 'king of the *Fionngall*' - from *Finn-gaill*, the Irish term for the Norse - can only be translated in this context as 'kings of the Hebridean Norse', but it has been taken to imply that the funeral of a Lord of the Isles followed the traditional burial rites of the Scots, Irish and Norse kings interred before them in the Reilig Odhrain.

Donald himself survived the battle and dedicated himself to his religious interests until his death c.1422. His monastic endowments are listed with his obituary in the *Book of Clanranald*.

Donald, son of John, married Mairi, daughter of the earl of Ross, and it is through her that the earldom of Ross came to Clan Donald.

He gave lands in Mull and in Islay to the monastery of Iona, and ... he made a covering of gold and silver for the relic of the hand of Columcille, and he himself took the brotherhood of the order.

He afterwards died in Islay, and his full noble body was interred on the south side of the Teampull Odhrain.

Donald of Harlaw was the last of the Lords of the Isles to be buried on Iona. His son and successor Alexander died in 1449 and was buried in the Cathedral of Fortrose, probably as a gesture in support of the Lordship's claim on Ross. Alexander's son John was to be the last Lord of the Isles. He surrendered the Lordship to James IV of Scotland in 1493 and died in poverty at Dundee in 1503. He was buried – at his own request – in Paisley Abbey.

With the death of the last Lord of the Isles the dynasty of Somerled passed from the pages of Scotland's story.

In its heyday, the seat of the Lordship had been at Finlaggan on Islay and there met the Council for the government of the Isles. The composition of the Council varied at different times, but its members represented the lesser branches of the house of Somerled, each with its own lands held under the Lordship and each with its history complicated as much by marriage as by ancient rivalry*. Different sources give different accounts of the composition of the Council of the Isles, but Dean Monro's version describes it as having been composed of twelve chieftains – amongst them the MacIan of Ardnamurchan, the Maclean of Duart and the Maclean of Lochbuie, the Macleod of Harris and the Macleod of Lewis, the MacNeil of Barra and the MacNeil of Gigha, the Macdonald of Kintyre and the Macdonald of Keppoch – under the presidency of the Lord of the Isles and attended also by the Bishop of the Isles and the Abbot of Iona.

Each of these chief families of the Isles had its claim to a tomb in the Reilig Odhrain, if not by right of descent from the house of Somerled then by right of marriage into Clan Donald. The *Book of Clanranald* provides one example in its note of John of Islay, first Lord of the Isles, that he had 'one daughter, **Mairi**'.

That Mairi was the wedded wife of Hector Maclean, Lord of Duart ... and she was interred in Iona in the church of the Black Nuns.

Martin Martin was able to identify very many of these tombs of the clans and to describe a number of the stones which he found on the ridge of the chieftains.

'There is a Heap of Stones without the Church', writes Martin, 'under which Mackean of Ardnamurchan lies buried.' Perhaps this was the John (Gael. *Eoin),* grandson of Somerled, who is identified by the Sleat historian as the forbear of the MacEans – or MacIans – buried on Iona.

---

* The history of the Lordship and clans of the Isles is too complex for summary here. Especially interested readers are referred to the further reading listed on p.127.

Of this John are descended the MacEans of Ardnamurchan. He was buried at Icolumkill.

'In the west end', observes Martin, 'is the Tomb of.Gilbrid', but whether or not this might be the burial-place of Gillebride, father of Somerled, is unknown.

The families of Mack-Lean of Duart, Loch-buy, and Coll, lie next all in Armour, as big as the Life.

This burial-ground of Clan Maclean contains casualties of celebrated Scottish battles who can be reliably identified from clan tradition. Two of them are Macleans of Duart who lie beneath the great stones carved with impressively detailed figures accoutred in the distinctive medieval battle-gear of the west Highlands - the high, conical helmet over a hood of chain mail, the long war-coat of quilted leather and the two-handed 'claymore' (Gael. *claidheamh-mor,* 'great sword').

Beneath this stone lay **Sallow Hector,** the ninth chief of the Macleans of Duart, who was slain, as was almost the entire Scots nobility beside their king James IV, at Flodden Field in 1513. Under the same stone was buried his ancestor and namesake, the **Red Hector Maclean of Duart** who fell fighting for the second Lord of the Isles at Harlaw in 1411. Another slab, carved with the tall-masted galley of the Macleans, is believed to mark the grave of the notorious sea-reiver **Alan of the Faggots,** the illegitimate son of a sixteenth-century Maclean of Duart and forbear of the Macleans of Torloisk.

Beside the tombs of the Macleans lay the stone carved with the Macleod galley, indicated by its low yard-arm, and the confirming inscription *Hic jacet ...*

MACLEAN OF DUART

120

M'Leoid. This stone had been earlier located near the gate to the Reilig Odhrain where it marked the grave of the heir to the Macleod of Lewis who fell in the battle fought off Tobermory c.1481 and remembered as the sea-fight of Bloody Bay. The battle was fought between the fleets of John, the last Lord of the Isles, and his rebellious son Angus, called 'Angus Og' and 'a bold, forward man and high-minded' according to the seannachies. This Angus Og had a great leaning to the old piratical ways and James IV held the Lord of the Isles responsible for his son's 'rebellis and traitouris'. The clans of Maclean, Macleod and MacNeil came to the support of the Lordship, but the rest of Clan Donald brought out their war-galleys for Angus Og who was able to claim the victory at Bloody Bay. It was this battle which effectively destroyed John's authority in the Isles and eventually brought about his surrender of the ruined Lordship to King James.

One more Maclean - whose gravestone on Iona shows him buckling on his great sword - is sufficiently celebrated, at least by tradition, to deserve mention here. This is the Maclean of Lochbuie called **'Ewen of the Little Head'** (Gael. *Eóghan a' Chinn Bhig)* who was slain in battle with his father in 1538, when - according to the seannachies - 'the scalp of his head was struck off in the combat'. The folklore of the Isle of Mull warns that when a Maclean of Lochbuie is about to die a headless horseman will be heard riding riot through the sky, 'Eóghan of the Little Head making much ado and uproar'.

The *Carmina Gadelica* includes fragments of Gaelic verse telling how, on the morning before his death, Ewen met a woman washing linen at a ford and asked her to foretell the outcome of the fray. 'She left a ban upon Eóghan of the Little Head that his ghost should be running before his people before the death of men and making hubbub and confusion above Loch Buie

MACLEAN OF LOCHBUY

122

whenever a MacLaine chief should die.'

This strange motif of the 'washer at the ford' is a legacy of the most ancient Irish tradition and closely similar legends would have been sung by their harper to the Sons of Erc a thousand years before. Very little of which can be in any measure accounted 'history'. The 'washer at the ford' is no less a creature of the mythos of the Gael than the 'Odhran laid in earth on I-Columcille', and that realm of 'ravens and black rain' is, perhaps, a fitting place to close an *Iona Book of the Dead*.

GENEALOGIES

Oswy begot Egfrith. He is the Egfrith who fought a battle against his cousin, who was king of the Picts named Bruide, and fell there with the whole strength of his army.

Nennius, *Historia Brittonum.*

The Blood-Kinship of Egfrith of Northumbria
and Bruide mac-Beli, king of Picts.

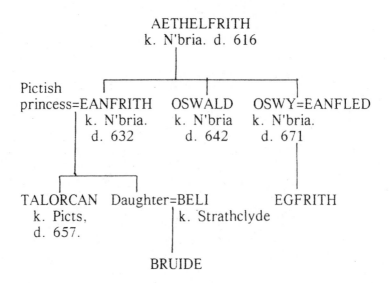

The Mac-Alpin Dynasty of Kings of Scots

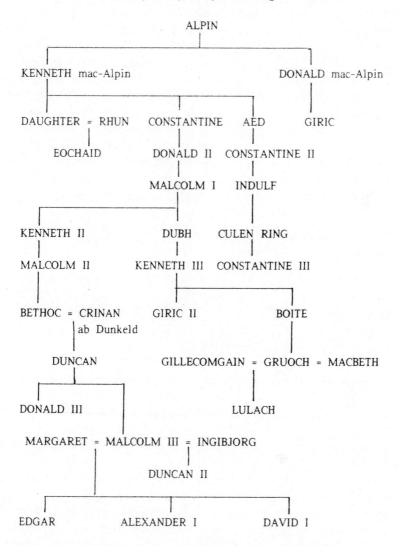

NB. This genealogy is greatly simplified and intended only to illustrate burials on Iona referred to in the foregoing text.

The Dynasty of Somerled and the Lordship of the Isles

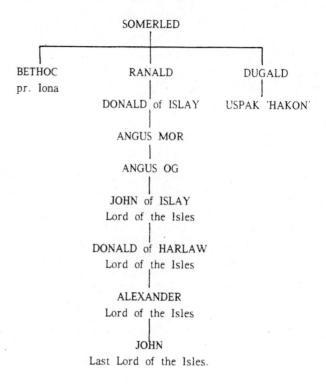

SOMERLED

BETHOC
pr. Iona

RANALD

DUGALD

DONALD of ISLAY

USPAK 'HAKON'

ANGUS MOR

ANGUS OG

JOHN of ISLAY
Lord of the Isles

DONALD of HARLAW
Lord of the Isles

ALEXANDER
Lord of the Isles

JOHN
Last Lord of the Isles.

NB. This genealogy is greatly simplified and intended only to illustrate burials on Iona referred to in the foregoing text.

FURTHER READING

Anderson, A. O.
    Scottish Annals from English Chroniclers AD 500–1286
                            Edinburgh, 1908; rev. Stamford, 1991.
    Early Sources of Scottish History AD 500–1286
                          2 vols. Edinburgh, 1922; rev. Stamford, 1990.
Anderson M.O.
    Kings & Kingship in Early Scotland
                            Edinburgh & London, 1980
Barrow, G. W. S.
    Kingship and Unity: Scotland 1000–1306
                        London, 1981; rev. Edinburgh, 1989
Byrne, F. J.
    Irish Kings & High-Kings
                                    London, 1973
Carmichael, Alexander
    Carmina Gadelica
              6 vols. Edinburgh, 1928; rep. 1 vol. Edinburgh 1992
Duncan, A. A. M.
    Scotland: The Making of the Kingdom
                               Edinburgh, 1975
Grant, I. F.
    The Lordship of the Isles
                    Edinburgh, 1935; rep. Edinburgh, 1983
Lynch, Michael
    Scotland: A New History
                                 London, 1991
Macquarrie, Alan
    Iona through the Ages
                                    Coll, 1983
Marsden, John
    Northanhymbre Saga: The History of the Anglo-Saxon Kings of
    Northumbria   London, 1992

Skene, W. F.
    Celtic Scotland: A History of Ancient Alban
                              3 vols. Edinburgh, 1886-90
Smyth, A. P.
    Warlords and Holy Men: Scotland AD 50-1000
                  London, 1984; rep. Edinburgh, 1989
Williams, Ronald
    The Lords of the Isles: The Clan Donald and early Kingdom
    of the : Scots   London, 1984

rev. revised edition
rep. reprint

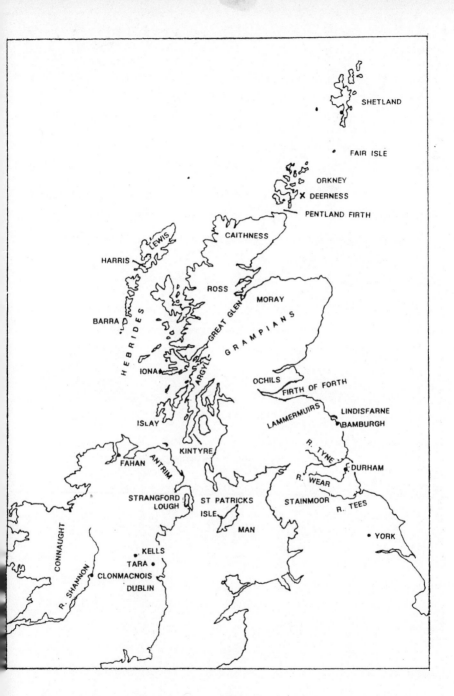

Also published by Llanerch:

JOHN OF FORDUN'S CHRONICLE OF THE SCOTTISH
NATION, a facsimile reprint, edited by W. F. Skene.

THE ANNALS OF TIGERNACH, Latin & Irish text with
intercalated English translations by Whitley Stokes, a
facsimile reprint from *Revue Celtique* 1896/7.

SAINT COLUMBA OF IONA by Lucy Menzies.

SAINT MARGARET, QUEEN OF SCOTLAND, by Lucy
Menzies.

TWO CELTIC SAINTS: NINIAN AND KENTIGERN, a
facsimile from the Historians of Scotland series.

LIVES OF THE SCOTTISH SAINTS: SERVANUS,
MAGNUS, QUEEN MARGARET by Turgot, and the
shorter life of SAINT COLUMBA by Cumine the Fair,
translated by W. Metcalfe.

For a complete list of 100+ titles, facsimile reprints and
small-press editions, writte to Llanerch Publishers,
Felinfach, Lampeter, Dyfed, SA48 8PJ.